FISHING SOFT BAITS IN SALTWATER

FISHING SOFT BAITS IN SALTWATER

Pete Barrett

Burford Books

Printed in the United States of America.

10   9   8   7   6   5   4   3   2   1

Library of Congress Cataloging-in-Publication Data
      Barrett, Peter.
      Fishing soft baits in saltwater / Pete Barrett.
            p.   cm.
      Includes index.
      ISBN 978-1-58080-148-5
      1. Soft baits.   2. Saltwater fishing.   I. Title.
SH451.4.B37   2008
799.16—dc22
                                        2007052466

DEDICATION

To my grandfather, Floyd Keyser, who loved fishing and lit the
flame of my fishing passion.

To my wife, Linda, who shares my love of fishing and always
catches the biggest fluke.

And, to my son, Rich, my favorite fishing buddy, who keeps the
flame lit. Grandpop Keyser would be thrilled.

CONTENTS

ACKNOWLEDGMENTS

For over 40 years, I've had the unique opportunity to meet and fish with many terrific people who enthusiastically shared their fishing tips and tricks, including their best techniques with soft-plastic lures. I hope this book helps to repay the debt I owe to the captains, guides, friends and fishermen who generously offered their advice and support. By passing along these fishing techniques, I hope others can use them and get more enjoyment from this wonderful sport of fishing.

I've particularly enjoyed spending time on the water with Captain Mark Nichols of D.O.A. Lures. He has a great sense of humor, plenty of opinions about everything, superb fishing skills and he thinks like a fish. He is a wonderful fishing companion, completely enjoying the day's fishing experience in good weather or bad, hot bite or slow pick. Mark provided plenty of inspiration for this book and I'm grateful for his friendship and patience as he taught me lots of good stuff.

Captain Jim White's *How to Fish Plastic Baits in Saltwater* was the first book to open the eyes of thousands of coastal fishermen to the many exciting soft-plastic lure-fishing techniques that have been so successful all along the coast. An accomplished writer and full-time captain (whiteghos1@aol.com), Jim dragged his freshwater guiding techniques into the salt chuck and we have all reaped the benefits of his expertise. He is a great guy to fish with, and his enthusiasm for fishing is boundless.

Many years ago, just before Al Reinfelder, creator of the Alou Bait Tail and Alou Eel, passed away in an accident on the Delaware River, I was blessed with an opportunity to share lunch with him and talk about how he used the Bait Tail and Alou Eel to make some amazing catches of striped bass. His Bait Tail fishing techniques are timeless and are just as effective today. Many of his techniques are sprinkled throughout this book and I continue to appreciate his guidance and enthusiasm for the striped bass.

Frank Johnson of Mold Craft Lures is a raconteur of sorts; quick with a tall tale (but always true!), he's also a great guy to fish with, and I was happy to spend time with him aboard his *Soft Head* trolling for blue marlin off Walkers Cay, Bahamas, many years ago. Over the following years, Frank freely gave of his advice, and to this day his squid daisy chains and Mold Craft trolling lures are a vital part of my offshore trolling spread. Always the great innovator, he was the first to create a fishable fake ballyhoo.

If Chuck Richardson had a buck for every natural ballyhoo bait he's rigged, he could retire handsomely! Chuck's company, Tournament Cable, showcases his inventive fishing mind with a unique array of off-shore products, many that now rely on soft-plastic ballyhoo baits for their success, including rigged ballyhoo, spreader bars, beautiful sail-fish and marlin dredges and much more. Chuck's help with the off-shore chapter was essential and I'm grateful for his help.

Recreational fishermen are besieged and surrounded on every side by wacky extreme environmentalists and an overbearing bureaucratic government with too many bizarre fisheries manage-ment schemes, so I'm especially grateful to Jim Donofrio, Executive Director of the Recreational Fishing Alliance, for his courage, good humor, hard work and perseverance. The RFA does a lot of the unpleasant grunt work in Washington that allows all of us to con-tinue fishing. My hat is off to Jim and the RFA crew.

INTRODUCTION

If your only game plan for fishing soft-plastic lures in saltwater is to drape a worm or shad body on a bucktail or leadhead and then cast away, you're missing out on some great fishing opportunities. Tear a few pages from your freshwater largemouth bass fishing cousin's book of tricks and try soft baits rigged Texas or Carolina style. You'll be pleasantly surprised with increased catches of fluke, weakfish and school stripers. No, you don't have to yell "Son!" every time you hook up, but there's no law against splitting your face with a big grin.

Split-tail minnow baits, curly tails, shad tails and traditional "rubber" worms can all be rigged using so-called freshwater methods to catch fish along the coast. These rigging methods are especially effective when light-tackle fishing in back-bay shallow water or shallow areas just inside coastal inlets. Bottom huggers like summer flounder, and tide-running weakfish and school stripers have a hard time resisting these seductive baits. Several unique rigging methods offer a wide range of retrieve options that cause the baits to flutter, dance and skip in a manner that fish find quite irresistible.

Soft plastics, usually called plastics or soft baits, are equally at home on the offshore grounds fooling yellowfin tuna on the troll or jigged near pods of bait, and at the edge of the surf where striped bass prowl in the Northeast, and tarpon and snook cruise the surf's edge in Florida. Bottom fishermen tease big grouper off southern reefs and steaker-size codfish off New England wrecks, and trolling with shads rigged on an umbrella rig is now a favorite, time-tested method that New Jersey charter skippers use to score good catches of striped bass. Sailfish catches can also improve dramatically when big plastic shads or ballyhoo are rigged on dredges to imitate a school of bait. Innovative fishermen have been developing unique and dramatically successful methods to help them catch more back-bay, coastal and offshore fish, and you're missing a good bet if you haven't spent more time learning about saltwater soft baits.

Fishing with soft-plastic baits has become an essential part of the saltwater tactics and techniques used by local pro fishermen, guides and charter captains, but many anglers still have not gone beyond the basics. The purpose of this book is to provide fish-proven information about how to select, rig and fish soft-plastic baits along the coast. It's a risky task, because new methods are rapidly introduced every season, which means some brand-new technique may be left out of this book on the very day it is printed. No matter, there is still plenty of solid info here, which can be used to experiment and develop even more new tactics. Like many anglers, I find new ways to rig and fish soft-plastic baits each season—and that's what adds a big dose of satisfaction to my fishing. Trying something new—and discovering that it works!—always adds to the overall fishing experience.

It's amazing to think how far we have come. Forty years ago the big decision when fishing a soft bait was choosing the color worm to drape on a bucktail. Today's decisions include selecting from a huge array of lure sizes, colors, shapes, actions, scents, rattles, hook styles and head shapes. The selection process can seem daunting.

There's also plenty of overlap in the various rigging and fishing techniques, which adds even more questions to the decision-making task. Most soft-plastic baits can be rigged and fished in several ways. Take the basic plastic worm; it can be rigged on a leadhead or a bucktail, or as a jigging teaser, trolled with double hooks and a spinner, or fished shallow as a Texas rig, or deep as a Carolina rig, or hooked in the middle as a wacky rig. The same rigging techniques also apply to jerkbaits, curly tails, shrimp and shads, and most other soft baits.

To keep things simple, this book is organized so it first covers the origins of these amazing lures, how they are made and the many types that are marketed today. Shifting into second gear, the basic rigging techniques that apply to all soft lures provides a great foundation from which to build the specialized chapters about rigging and fishing with leadhead and swimbaits, shrimp, Slug-Go baits, trolling shads and offshore lures. We'll finally up shift into high gear with the last two chapters which wrap up all the many tackle choices and a close look at the wide array of fishing techniques you'll need to score on your favorite gamefish.

I hope *Fishing Soft Baits in Saltwater* clears away some of the mystery and serves up a buffet of ideas to add a few more fish to your cooler.

Catch 'em up!

—Pete Barrett

FISHING SOFT BAITS IN SALTWATER

1

THE ULTIMATE
SALTWATER LURE

Soft-plastic baits are the ultimate saltwater lure. That's a pretty tall statement, but it's true. No other family of lures can match the versatility, feel, realism and fish-catching appeal of soft baits, and by varying the size, color, shape, hook style and leadhead, soft-plastic lures or baits can be retrieved with a wide variety of fish-catching techniques. They fool fish when worked as surface lures, at mid-depth ranges and down into the deep.

Pick most any soft-plastic lure; a worm, shad, jerkbait, tube bait or curly tail, and by modifying the way it is rigged, it can be cast, trolled, jigged, popped and jerked to imitate virtually any imaginable natural bait. Retrieved seductively slow, they fool snook and stripers. Stomp on the accelerator for a super-quick retrieve and you'll get eager strikes from jacks and bluefish. At mid-range speeds, they fool weakfish, sea trout and redfish, and they can be crawled along the bottom at a snail's pace for croaker, fluke and flounder.

Despite their enormous versatility, many saltwater fishermen have barely scratched the surface of the soft-plastic lure's full potential. Depending upon where they fish, many coastal anglers simply stick with the basic popular soft-plastic lures that are sold in local tackle shops. If pink shads are the hot bait for reds or trout, that's what everyone locally will fish—it's no wonder that's what the fishing reports say is the "hot" lure; it's the only lure being fished!

But there's a potential problem when you only fish with the local hot-shot lure. What will you do about those days when the water is cloudy, or the water temperature falls, or the wind is against the tide, or too much boat traffic puts the fish down, or it's too hot, or too cold? What then? You have to break out of the box and try some new ideas and fishing techniques to stay at the top of your game.

There are tons of ways to fish soft baits; techniques that often go far beyond the locally popular basics, and these innovative techniques will help you score fish when the standard stuff fails to produce. That's when this book will add a few more fish to your cooler, or help you catch that trophy, or make it possible to release a few more fish while your buddies are scratching their heads wondering how come you're hooking up so many more fish than they are. Trying new ideas will definitely get some extra fish smell on your hands, and put some added spark and excitement into your fishing.

There are great similarities, but fishing soft-plastic lures in the salt is not as simple as fishing in freshwater. The coastal environment has tides and currents to deal with that are unlike anything found in a freshwater pond or lake. Stream and creek fishing is somewhat similar to saltwater fishing, in terms of water movement, but only a very large freshwater river can come close to duplicating the sheer magnitude of the powerful currents triggered by daily tidal changes of the ocean.

Saltwater anglers not only deal with seasonal fish migrations, but also the daily migrations of many saltwater gamefish as water temperatures, tides, weather and changes from daylight to night influence bait and gamefish. These daily migrations often occur over a distance of several miles.

If you have not yet gone beyond the basics of soft-plastic lure fishing, you'll enjoy trying some of the many techniques found in these pages. If you're a skeptic, keep in mind that these lures, rigging techniques and fishing methods are used every day by professional guides, charter captains and local sharpies. These folks didn't get to be good

Many coastal fishermen consider soft-plastic baits the ultimate saltwater lure. They can be fished shallow or deep and come in a huge array of colors, sizes and actions to catch striped bass, snook, weakfish, jacks, cobia, tarpon, fluke and sea trout.

anglers by relying on techniques that don't catch fish. Their fishing methods and soft-plastic rigging techniques will work for you, too.

Most of these ideas aren't anything new, but they may be new to the area where you fish local to home. I recall a story a good friend and fishing buddy, Eric Burnley, once told me about D.O.A. Lure creator Mark Nichols when the two were fishing the Chesapeake Bay-Bridge Tunnel for striped bass in early fall. Eric used his favorite local lures while Mark fished his own D.O.A. favorites. Although fishing new water, Mark caught as many or more fish than Eric because he had confidence in his product and absolutely knew his techniques would work just as well at the mouth of Chesapeake Bay as they had at the mouth of the expansive St. Lucie Inlet in his home waters of Stuart, Florida. It proves the point that a good lure, fished with the right technique, will catch fish anywhere—off Cape Cod, Montauk Point, Oregon Inlet, Charleston Harbor or Key West.

SOFT-PLASTIC ADVANTAGES

There are many significant advantages to fishing with soft-plastic baits. They embody the ultimate in realism with soft and flexible bodies that feel alive when a gamefish strikes. They can be manufactured in thousands of shapes to provide a limitless variety of size, silhouette and action options; and they come in color schemes that include vivid attractor palettes and the much more subtle hues that identically imitate the real thing.

Depending on the manufacturer's molding formula, soft-plastic baits will have a density that makes them float, suspend with neutral buoyancy or sink. Each of these characteristics can be used to add to their realism and fish attractiveness. They are amazingly versatile and can be rigged in dozens of ways with hundreds of minute variations. Slipped onto a leadhead, rigged without a weight on a single hook, trolled with a skirt draped over the body or jigged deep as a teaser above a diamond jig, the variations are virtually without limit.

An added bonus is the many ways in which soft plastics can be presented to fool gamefish. High or low, shallow or deep, fast or slow, aggressive action or minimal action, soft-plastics can be manipulated in every conceivable way.

A buddy and I fished one morning just inside Barnegat Inlet catching school stripers at the first hint of pink in the dawn May sky, then had action with weakfish on the flats at Tice's Shoal at sun up, finally switching to bottom fishing for fluke near the BB Marker by 9 a.m.—and we caught all our fish on the same soft-plastic lures. Only the colors of the tails changed. The bass hit chartreuse Fin-S Fish fished deep along the sedge bank, the weakies hit bubble gum pink fished in just 8 feet of water, and the fluke fell in love with silver flecked Fin-S Fish jigged vertically in 12 feet of water. Try this with a top-water swimmer, a popper or a metal jig. You can't! Many lures are great for one style of fishing, but soft plastics can be fished in virtually every fishing situation imaginable.

What could feel more realistic than a soft lure? Even a spooky, tentative fish will not be aware the lure is a fake when it bites down on a bait that has the feel of a real live natural bait. Captain John Kumiski, who guides in Florida's Indian River Lagoon, told me that short-striking redfish will repeatedly hit a soft lure until they finally get ticked off enough to eat the entire lure and get hooked. I saw this myself with weakfish one morning in New Jersey's Barnegat Bay when a slow retrieve would get hit four or five times before the fish finally got hooked. I can only imagine the weakfish thinking, "This thing looks real, feels real, so why can't I kill it?" With one more aggressive lunge, the frustrated weakfish makes one more swipe and is hooked. "Oops, that was a mistake," but it's too late by then.

Soft-plastic lures feel like the real thing to spooky redfish—like this one caught by Florida Sportsman *editor Jeff Weakly—and they're ideal for inshore and back-bay light-tackle fishing.*

Soft plastics can also be molded to match any size, silhouette or shape of a real bait. The slender Fin-S Fish looks like a sand eel or spearing, the rounder paddle tail baits look like mullet, the deep-body profile of a shad looks just like a bunker, herring or pilchard, a freshwater bass worm is also a dead ringer for a saltwater sea worm, the Mister Twister looks like any lively bait swimming naturally and there are soft-plastic lures that look like mackerel, skipjack, squid, shrimp and crabs.

Actions vary widely with plastic baits. The paddle-tail, shad tail and Mister Twister-style soft baits have a built-in action, while other plastics have no action of their own. The paddle tail and shad tail, with their rapid wiggling side-to-side tail action, create a visual stimulus and transmit a natural vibrating sound into the water. Same goes for the Mister Twister or curly-tail baits with their wiggling, twisting tails that reflect light and pulsate seductively. Besides the visual attraction of these baits, the rapid pulsating of the tails emits vibrations into the water that fish can also home in on for the strike.

Other plastics, such as squids, shrimp, crabs, worms and slender jerkbaits have no action of their own, and rely entirely on the angler to twitch, jerk or sweep the rod tip to create the illusion of something alive. The action of these lures is limited only by the angler's own imagination. Watch a live squid in a chum slick and you will notice that it swims slow and steady, almost floating, but it will dart quickly to grab a chunk of bait. This swimming action can be exactly duplicated with a fake soft-plastic squid. Shrimp have a similar free-floating natural swimming movement as they "walk" close to the bottom of shallow grass beds. A slow retrieve with short twitches of the rod tip will make the artificial shrimp look just like a live, natural bait and trout, stripers, snook, redfish—even bonefish—will eagerly eat them.

Color combinations with soft plastics are limited only by the imagination of the manufacturer, and they include bright attractors such as pink, chartreuse and yellow to subtle blends that look so

Weakfish are easy marks for an artificial shrimp worked over a shallow grass bed, or for a leadhead fished deep along a channel edge.

realistic you'd swear the bait would swim away if you dropped it in the water! There are also the traditional purple, black and dark brown colors that score big time catches. Captain Brian Horsley of the Outer Banks swears by root beer for summer sea trout and TV host Blair Wiggins echoes that opinion by calling root beer his "go-to" color for snook. In the Northeast surf, the jumbo-size Slug-Go in jet black is one of East Coast surf-sharpie DJ Muller's favorites, saying, "The guys in Rhode Island showed me a few rigging tricks with the black Slug-Go and it is even more deadly than a live eel when fished right."

IN THE BEGINNING

The earliest soft-plastic creations were literally home-made in a garage or basement workshop, or at the kitchen table. DeLong Lures poured their first soft bait in 1945, but Nick Crème is generally credited with being the first to popularize the soft-plastic worm starting in 1949. DeLong Lures and Crème Lures are both still going strong with a wide collection of present-day products—a testament to their brilliant innovation and creativity.

Until the 1960s, soft baits were used primarily by freshwater largemouth bass fishermen. Florida's snook and trout anglers began adding worms to their bucktails for increased action and their northern counterparts did the same for striped bass and weakfish. By the early 1970s, if you weren't fishing a white-bucktail-and-purple-worm combo for Cape May weakfish, you just weren't fishing. Local hot colors and bucktail combinations flourished all along the coast.

Pete Foley of Boone Baits told me his company began marketing leadheads with shrimp-like soft tails in the late 1950s. In Florida, the Boone Trout Tout gained a mighty strong following before the soft-plastic craze ever began to sweep along the coast. For many salty anglers, a little education from peers and tackle shop owners was needed before soft lures would gain their full popularity.

I was lucky to have several learning opportunities with soft-plastic lures for Jersey stripers, Virginia sea trout and Florida snook starting about 40 years ago. Like many saltwater fishermen at that time, I was a traditional bucktail, surface popper or swimming plug believer, and did not fish with soft-plastic baits at all. I was also just starting out in a life of fishing adventures and needed a lot of coaching to try new things. Paul Siciliano, the friendly owner of the long-gone Monmouth Bait and Tackle Shop, was the first to prod me toward soft plastic lures when he urged me to try an Alou Bait Tail for fishing along New Jersey's rocky jetties at Long Branch, Deal and Asbury Park just below Sandy Hook. As a young guy with lots to learn, the Bait Tail helped me gain much needed experience catching striped bass.

Al Reinfelder's Bait Tail and Alou Eel were among the early successful saltwater soft-plastic lures. His book Bait Tail Fishing *is a collector's item.*

The Bait Tail was the creation of Al Reinfelder and his fishing buddy Lou Palma. They put their heads together to create an ingenious lure, which was nothing more than a simple leadhead jig with a soft-plastic tail. Careful design blended with on-the-water fishing experience made the Bait Tail so versatile it could be cast from jetties, worked from bridges or cast from a boat. Like Pinocchio's papa Gepetto, the angler had to breathe life into the lure to add action to make the jig dance enticingly; although at times, no action at all was the most deadly way to fool striped bass.

Along with the famous Alou Eel, the Bait Tail opened the eyes of many a hard-core bass fanatic to the promise of soft-plastic baits. Al's long-out-of-print book, *Bait Tail Fishing*, is a treasure trove of fishing information and copies are still in great demand with fishing book collectors and cherished by knowledgeable fishermen. If you find one at a fishing flea market, an antiques shop or listed with a collectible fishing book dealer, buy it no matter the cost because it is probably one of the best fishing investments you will ever make. The Bait Tail was my very first exposure to soft-plastic baits in saltwater and it fooled many striped bass for this neophyte jetty hopper.

Soon after, while stationed at Little Creek, Virginia's Naval Amphib School, I was fortunate to fish Lynnhaven Inlet several times a week right near the old drawbridge for speckled sea trout. The hot bait used by local sharpies was the Bagley's Salty Dawg, a leadhead lure with a soft-plastic body that vaguely resembled the shape and silhouette of a shrimp. My catches improved after I hooked-up with a Navy chief petty officer from the base, who helped me figure out the best times and tides. His favorite Salty Dawg had a white head and a pink plastic tail. The sea-trout action was predictably very good on a falling tide while wading along the sandy beach near the bridge at dawn and dusk. Spike trout of only 2 or 3 pounds made up most of the catch, but school striped bass and summer flounder also ate the jig, and sometimes bluefish.

Another year later and back on board with the Garcia Tackle Company, I was sent on a late-May fishing trip to Stuart, Florida. The snook fishing at the inlet was absolutely amazing, and the mixed bag of species from the three-day trip included speckled sea trout, a small tarpon, a variety of snappers and grouper, lookdowns, ladyfish and plenty of big crevalle jacks. The two hot lures were the Boone Trout Tout, which my guide used, and the Alou Bait Tail, which I used, because it had just come under the Garcia banner as part of a comprehensive line of lures being created by Al Reinfelder as he made the transition to expand his creative horizons with the corporate fishing tackle giant. Although we did fall back on live bait by mid morning, the best action each day was at sun-up on the soft-plastic lures. Man, did they catch fish!

Sarasota guide Captain Rick Grassett catches redfish, trout and snook on artificial shrimp, including big 'gator trout like this one he caught along the edge of a drop-off.

By the early 1970s soft-plastic baits were soaring in popularity, fueled by the huge explosion of weakfish that brought the return of these great gamefish from Rhode Island's Narragansett Bay to Delaware Bay and Chesapeake Bay in the south. Trout Touts, Salty Dawgs and Bait Tails saw competition from traditional bucktails draped with purple worms, and the introduction of the remarkable Mister Twister tail. Coastal fishermen were buying soft baits by the bagful and the popularity of soft-plastic baits was firmly established. In the span of a mere 10 years, from the late 1960s to the 1970s, soft-plastic lures evolved from being relatively unknown in the salt to becoming a must-have lure that no self-respecting saltwater angler would be without.

Today the trend continues and it's rare to find a coastal fisherman without at least several soft lures in his tackle bag. Tackle shops have walls jam-packed with an enormous variety of plastics, and many guides have come to rely on soft plastics as their primary lures, not even using fresh-dead or live bait unless absolutely necessary. While fishing with Captain Rick Grassett, a premier guide from the Sarasota, Florida area, he confided, "On many days I only fish D.O.A. shrimp rather than the real deal and catch just as many, if not more, snook, redfish and trout." Rick's not alone. Many guides believe the imposters are just as good as the natural shrimp baits.

WHAT IS THIS STUFF?

From the very first worm, soft plastics had a rubbery feel and to this day, many anglers nickname soft-plastic baits as "rubber" baits. They aren't rubber at all, however, the name has stuck and when a New England surfcaster says he's fishing the "rubbah" he's casting a soft-plastic Slug-Go or Hogy bait. Likewise, an inshore coastal caster is still likely to say he's fishing a bucktail and "rubber" worm for weakfish, striped bass or snook, just because old nicknames sometimes hang on tight and won't let go.

Soft-plastic baits are most often made of polyvinyl chloride (PVC), which in its most basic form is the same stuff used to make the ubiquitous white plastic pipes for household plumbing, and it's the same stuff used for automobile and boat parts, vinyl house siding, sprinkler systems, kids toys, electrical components, household appliances and thousands of other items we use in our daily lives. PVC is found literally everywhere in our lives. Through changes in the chemical formulas, the material is made soft and pliable and is therefore quite different in its final molecular composition than harder versions of PVC products.

My long-time fishing buddy, Jerry Gomber, heads up product development for Bimini Bay's Tsunami lures and tackle, and I turned to him to get the skinny on how soft-plastic lures are actually made.

PVC is generally clear when heated and can readily be mixed with dyes and coloring agents to achieve almost any color variation. To get a fish-scale finish, it can be blended with metallic micro particles or slightly larger metallic flakes. To make floating formulas, micro balloons of air-like material can be added, as can fish scents and exotic scents that chemists believe will enhance the fish attraction of the finished lure. A special instrument, known as a durometer gauge, is used to test the relative softness of a prototype lure and once the manufacturer gets the right mix, that formula can be duplicated thousands of times with no variation in quality.

By mixing and heating special, carefully-guarded proportions of PVC and the oil-based chemicals specified by the factory's chemist, manufacturers are able to brew a gooey soup of liquid plastic that when cooled makes their lures take on the attributes of flexibility, durability and texture. There is no "right" mixture; some lures are made softer for a more life-like feel, but they give up some durability as a trade-off for that softness. Others are blended with a mixture that increases their durability, with a corresponding decrease in flexibility. These qualities of softness and durability can also be custom blended into one lure, such as the Mann's Bait Company Hardhead series with a head that has a tough tear-resistant PVC blend to better hold onto the hook, and a softer blend at the tail end of the bait for maximum flexibility.

Manufacturers receive PVC in barrels of soft nuggets that must first be melted, or in 55-gallon drums of a milky liquid that has to be heated. The material is made hot enough to have the correct flow rate so it can be pressure injected into molds, allowed to cool and then

Heated PVC is liquefied and then injected into molds that make dozens of lures at a time. After cooling in a water bath, the lures are separated and made ready for packaging.

removed from the mold. Each mold is capable of producing a dozen or more soft-plastic lures on a "tree." If you built plastic models when you were a kid, you'll remember how all the parts were held together on a parts tree and you'd snap off the part you needed at each stage of the model's construction. Soft-plastic lures look much the same. The individual lure bodies are cut off by a molding technician, the excess plastic is trimmed and the lures are then made ready for rigging and final packaging.

A limited number of manufacturers use the hand-poured method instead of injection molding. This is a much slower production process, but one which allows the manufacturer to do some wonderful, creative blending of colors, and for this reason the hand-poured lures have a strong following among specialty manufacturers and fishermen that need something unique.

Swimbaits are injection molded around a leadhead, sometimes with a holographic flash foil inserted, and are usually made from clear PVC. The finishes are painted onto the lure with special paints that will permanently adhere to the oily surface of soft PVC baits.

Many anglers appreciate PVC's ability to repair easily. A bait ripped and slashed by a toothy bluefish or barracuda can be repaired on the spot with a drop of cyanoacrylate glue (aka CA glue), like the so-called super glues sold in hobby shops, hardware and craft stores. This can be a very important factor when you're down to the last shad in your bag and the striped bass are only hitting that one hot color. A quick repair can save the tide.

Although PVC is the material of choice for most soft baits, manufacturers are experimenting with new formulas and new materials, such as Cyber-Flexxx, which is based upon a crystal-gel compound. It offers extreme flexibility with a unique ability to stretch without breaking. Cyber-Flexxx is less affected by wicked bluefish, Spanish mackerel or barracuda teeth, and is more buoyant than PVC so it "floats" better when fishing in shallow water.

Other companies are experimenting with plastisol, a compound that has excellent flex properties and which is non-toxic to the environment.

Then there is Berkley, a division of Pure Fishing, with its amazing Gulp! soft baits. This product is a 100% natural blend of secret stuff that is flexible, durable and with a unique ability to emit scent into the water 400 times faster than any other man-made scent formula. This stuff feels just like other soft-plastic baits, but it is a natural substance, biodegradable and with an amazingly powerful scent attractor. Initially targeted for freshwater anglers, Berkley has expended the lineup to include all the favorite saltwater scents and shapes; squid, shrimp, sand fleas, peeler crabs, sea

Berkley's Gulp! soft baits feel like plastic, but are a natural biodegradable product with a powerful scent that calls in fish strikes.

worms, clams and more. This unique soft bait has become very popular with saltwater anglers.

Gulp! took over 12 years of research, experimentation and product development until becoming a reality under the expertise of project leader, John Proknow. As John put it when I met him at the Pure Fishing's Spirit Lake, Iowa research center, "These new baits are the difference between prime rib and a hot dog, and Gulp! is 70 percent more effective than a natural bait." Many guides and charter skippers agree, and Gulp! has a huge following with coastal anglers.

It's a tremendous breakthrough in artificial bait technology. Because it is water based, it disperses a powerful scent trail much faster than plastic baits. Gulp! looks, swims, smells, feels and tastes more natural to game fish than any plastic bait. It's so close to the real thing that fish actually eat it!

SCENTS

We know that fish have a highly developed sense of smell so adding a natural scent to a bait can only make it a better bait. Scents can be injected into the plastic formula at the time of manufacture, or scent can be added later by the angler by smearing the bait with a paste, jelly, oil or and spray application. Which type of add-on scent you use depends on your own preference and how long you need the scent to last. Oils generally wash off quickly, gels and pastes last longer. Oils are easier to use with lures that have a hollow chamber able to be filled with a cotton ball. Oils are also the best choice for storing lures overnight for the next day's fishing.

Many soft-bait anglers store their plastic tails in resealable plastic bags overnight after squirting an ounce or so of squid, shrimp, bunker or fish oil scent into the bag. Come morning, the lures will have absorbed the scent and be ready for action on the first cast. They will usually hold the scent for a longer time than the same soft bait that has been rubbed with scent oil only a few moments prior to fishing. All applied scents will wash off; some faster than others, so the scent should be re-applied after a dozen or so casts.

Hollow lures, like tube lures and the D.O.A. Baitbuster and Swimming Mullet, have body cavities that can be filled with paste or gel, or a cotton ball that will absorb an oil scent. Hollow bodies can hold scent for a long time and will call in several strikes before washing out.

Guides often use a short strip of scent-soaked felt (about an inch will do) and drape it on the hook above the soft bait. It will last for many casts and disperse the scent very effectively. When the scent is gone, squeeze the felt dry between your fingers and re-apply another dose of oil, paste or gel to keep the lure at its maximum potential.

Fish scents are packaged as oils, sprays and gels for a variety of easy applications. Select natural scents like shrimp, clam, crab, baitfish and squid for best results.

Lures with a molded-in scent will disperse a fish-attracting smell for the longest time. Bass Assassin, Berkley PowerBaits, D.O.A. Lures, Lunker City, Mann's Baits, Mister Twister Exude and PRADCO'S YUM baits are good examples, and there are many other similar baits sold at tackle shops with scent as part of their essential fish-catching abilities. On the freshwater scene, unusual scents like licorice, garlic and pumpkin are faddishly popular, but in coastal waters, the preference is for natural scents such as squid, sea worm, crab, shrimp and oily fish like bunker, mackerel and mullet.

Research at Pure Fishing has shown that the unusual scents often have the opposite affect and may actually repel fish! Stick with squid, anchovy, bunker, shrimp and the other naturals and you will probably catch more fish.

THE IMPORTANCE OF COLOR

One of the biggest advantages when fishing with soft-plastic baits is the virtually limitless variation of color combinations that is available. Choosing the right color is always an important decision as we start the fishing day. Do we select a color that has worked on previous days, or that is popular in the latest fishing reports? Are there other factors that come into play?

Three conditions have a major influence on the ability of a color to effectively convince a fish to strike; water clarity, depth and ambient light. In murky water, a lure's ability to reflect its color is substantially minimized, and as a fish's ability to see becomes restricted, it relies more on its ability to pick up vibrations through the lateral line. Bright lures, such as pink and chartreuse, will usually get more strikes in murky water simply because the lure is more visible, not because it resembles anything alive in nature.

A lure's color is dependent upon how well it reflects that color's wave lengths back to the eye of the fish or the angler. Red is seen as red because it reflects the red wave lengths back to the eye, while absorbing the other wave lengths of green, blue and yellow.

Something else to consider when choosing lure color: since the color of a lure is based upon light waves reflecting off its surface, for any color to exist, light waves must be able to penetrate below the surface, but not all wave lengths penetrate water equally. In fact, some wave lengths do not penetrate very deeply into the water at all. Red ceases to exist as a color only a few feet below the surface because its light waves can penetrate only a few feet. By comparison, chartreuse light waves deeply pierce the water and the lure will, therefore, reflect more of its color even at depths up to 30 feet below the surface.

This teen-size snook ate a bright pink-and-chartreuse electric chicken shad tail for Captain Charlie Fornabio while fishing just inside the St. Lucie Inlet.

When choosing lure colors, we also have to consider that in the fish's watery world, a lure's color does not appear the same as when held in the angler's hand out of the water. The greenish-blue tint of the water alters the underwater appearance of every color. The white shad takes on a pale blue-green tint along the beach or a pale brown tint in back bays because of the natural hue of the water. Yellow, pink and chartreuse become slightly greener in appearance beneath the water's surface. Dark colors are less influenced by the ambient tint of the water.

Some colors imitate natural bait; others serve as attractors only and have no apparent relation to anything that swims in the ocean. Chartreuse is a favorite color, but I can't recall ever seeing a chartreuse baitfish, squid or sea worm. Those bright colors, however, can be reflected for brief moments from many different baits. Carefully watch small bait, such as a quiet time when you are wade fishing, and as they dart you may see momentary flashes of gold or silver and of several bright colors, including chartreuse, yellow, pink and pale blue. Even though the bait does not always reflect pink, let's say, the fact that it does momentarily reflect pink as it quickly turns and darts may be enough to make a pink soft lure a deadly offering. While snorkeling, I've seen pods of squid that reflected pink, gold, red and blue, yet when a live one is dropped on the deck of a boat, the bright colors quickly fade and all we see is a whitish, brown dead bait. We must think in terms of what the fish sees in his natural environment, not what we see outside the fish's vision.

Most of the time, bright colors probably trigger a strike response because they are highly visible to the fish; such as in the summer season when back-bay waters experience algae and plankton blooms by the billions and make the water murky, or when rain waters wash mud from nearby rivers and salt creeks. The bright chartreuse, pink, yellow or white lure can readily be seen, so it gets the strikes.

When discussing lure color we must also consider the "flash" factor. Again, observing bait in its natural environment, as pods of bait swim, turn, dart and move, they reflect flashes of gold and silver. One morning in Connecticut's Norwalk Harbor, a huge school of 1-pound bunker looked like a mass of glittering, shimmering gold jewels. Is it any wonder that soft-plastic lures with a gold tint were the hot ticket that morning for striped bass along the Norwalk Islands and marshes? On another morning, a mass of glass minnows just inside Florida's Jupiter Inlet flashed brilliant silvery sparkles every time the school turned in its fast-paced morning commute along the sea wall. A soft-plastic tail with silver speckles was the bait of choice for nearby snook.

Flash is important. Even if the fish does not see the lure's color very well, it will often see the lure's flash, and this will trigger the strike. A

Fat or skinny, short or long, adding sparkle flakes to the soft bait during the molding process will make the lure flash brightly and attract more strikes.

bright, flashy lure is, therefore, often a great choice. Swimbaits, which we'll discuss later, take flash to the highest level with built-in metallic holographic foil inserts that flash with amazing brightness.

Why Fish Bite

Hunger? Anger? Territory protection? What triggers a fish to strike a lure is a question anglers have asked since ancient man dangled bone hooks at the water's edge. For centuries mankind had only SWAG technology to rely upon, but Scientific Wild Ass Guesses are being replaced by in-depth study and observation. The results are the next best thing to actually asking the fish, "Why did you eat that?"

Hunger is a primary reason why a fish strikes a soft-plastic lure. Fish are opportunistic feeders and in that context, they are always "hungry" and ready to eat. Whether they eat, or not, depends on the fish's responses to its senses of hearing, smell and sight.

Fish respond to sound, and since water carries sound much faster and for greater distances in water, fish actually hear very well. Loud, unusual sounds like a paddle banging the bottom of a kayak or flats skiff, or a lead sinker smacking the deck of a skiff will have a negative effect on nearby fish. However, there is a symphony of natural underwater sounds, such as the clicking of shrimp and crabs, crashing surf and tumbling rocks in a stream, or sounds from nearby fish. Fish also hear, or feel, vibrations in the water, such as the panicked twisting and turning of baitfish, the pulsating tail beats of tuna fish and the deep booming of a powerful swipe of a striped bass's tail. Far from silent, their aquatic environment is actually quite noisy.

The ears of a fish lie beneath the skin, but function in much the same manner as other animals. Fish also have a lateral line along their sides, a highly developed addition to their sensory nervous system that allows them to pick up pulsing vibrations in the water. The lateral line, therefore, picks up movement in the water, such as the rapid pulsating of a fast-vibrating curly tail lure.

Fish smell. Just ask your wife when you come home after knocking the stripers silly in the surf. Okay, but we're talking here about a fish's ability to smell odors in the water, a highly developed skill which is far superior to a human's. Jack Casey, a marine biologist who specialized in shark studies, once used the analogy that if a mako shark were a human, it could smell and locate someone smoking a pipe in a football stadium filled with thousands of sports fans. Because fish have enhanced smell capabilities, fishing soft-plastic lures with molded-in scent, or adding scents, is an important consideration.

Most game fish have the ability to see very well, but their vision may be restricted by murky water, the lack of daylight penetration in deep water or the lack of sunlight at night. The shape of their eye lens, and its ability to flatten and expand, allows the fish to focus, but since most fish have eyes on the sides of the heads, not in front as with humans, they do not have great depth perception. In fact most fish have a blind spot just in front of their nose. Ever wonder how an aggressive striped bass or snook can make several swipes at a lure and not get hooked? It's the blind spot. The fish loses sight of the lure at the last instant just before it strikes.

Using just the right combination of action, scent, color, and size helped Steven Merrill and his IGFA-rep dad, Jeff, hook up with this keeper fluke.

Dr. Keith Jones at the Pure Fishing Aquatic Research Center in Spirit Lake, Iowa has carefully studied the feeding habits and strike responses of largemouth bass in such detail that he can almost think like a bass. His book, *Knowing Bass* has become a classic data base of information tournament fishermen rely upon. Some of it can be applied to develop saltwater fishing strategies. Thirty years ago, Mark Sosin and John Clark wrote *Through the Fish's Eye*, a book that proved to be a revelation for many anglers intent on learning more about their fresh and saltwater quarry. Latest in the line of how-to-figure-out-fish books is Dr. David Rose's *The Fisherman's Ocean*, a book that combines fish sense with marine habitat.

All three books provide an amazing glimpse into the watery world of fish and help solve the daily riddle of "Why fish bite?" Check your local bookstore to get a copy of *Knowing Bass* by Dr. Keith A. Jones, published by The Lyons Press, PO Box 480, Guilford, CT 06437,

The Fisherman's Ocean by Dr. David A. Ross, published by Stackpole Books, 5067 Ritter Rd., Mechanicsburg, PA 17055. *Through the Fish's Eye* by Mark Sosin and John Clark has been out of print for many years, but copies can be found at used book stores, flea markets and used fishing book exhibits at sports shows. If you can find a copy, buy it—it's pure gold.

PUTTING IT ALL TOGETHER

Whether or not a fish will strike a soft-plastic lure or bait is usually the result of a chain of events, triggered first by the fish's response to sound. A lure with built-in action, such as a paddle tail, or a rattle that will transmit sounds and vibrations, can attract the attention of a striped bass, redfish, sea trout or flounder. Lures with built-in rattles will often get more strikes than lures with no sound device. Lures with a strong pulsating action can at times be more effective than a slow-swimming lure. It's the sound, or the feel of the lure's action and vibrations, that can trigger the first stage of a game fish's feeding response.

After sound catches the fish's attention, smell may take over in the second stage of the strike. A chum slick of ground mossbunker, grass shrimp or chunks of butterfish, can attract fish from far distances and call them to the boat and within casting range of a soft

The author caught this 6-pound summer flounder in 35 feet of water on a 1-ounce leadhead draped with a chartreuse soft-plastic shad tail soaked overnight in squid oil.

lure. Once close to the lure, individual lure scents will take over. A bucktail dressed with a worm or shad tail that has built-in scent will appeal to this second stage of a fish's feeding response because of the odor the bait emits into the water.

Scents have a powerful influence over fish, and that's why many knowledgeable fishermen enhance the appeal of their soft-plastic lures by squirting a drop or two of concentrated fish smell onto the lure or the bucktail hair. Soft plastic baits capable of emitting natural, fish-attracting odors into the water are usually better fish catchers than their odorless cousins.

The final stage of the strike is visual. After sound and smell have gotten the fish's attention, the game fish must use its eyes to make the final attack. With soft-plastic lures, the final stage of the strike can be affected by action, color or flash. Whether a fish strikes the lure or not, is also dependent upon the color, silhouette and visual appeal of the bait and how natural it looks.

The soft-plastic lure's action must be realistic. A fast wiggling shad tail looks like a baitfish and will get strikes, but that same lure with a fouled hook or a weed will not look natural and will not get strikes. The old adage of dark days, dark lures; bright day, bright lures, may or may not be true. Color contrast can be more important. A black Slug-Go works well because it is dramatically silhouetted against the sky and a striped bass can easily see its visual appeal. A bright flashy lure does the same thing—presents a clearly visible target for the fish to strike. In murky water, bright colors often get more strikes because they are simply more visible to the fish.

Some days the fishing is so easy, game fish will strike at anything you toss at them. That's the kind of day when every Joe Average can fill the cooler and have a great day fishing. Winning tournament fishermen, professional guides and charter captains, however, know that those days are blessings to be cherished, not counted on. Being a top-notch fisherman requires additional thinking when the fish seem to get lockjaw and stop feeding, and won't respond as expected. It's those times that the best fishermen try to think like a fish.

An off day can be saved by changing lure color from bright to dark, or to a flashy holographic finish. Lure actions can be changed by switching from a slow-swimming soft-plastic to a deep-running plastic. Shallow divers can be replaced by deep divers, and even the lure's profile can be changed from slim to chubby, short to long.

We may never know exactly why a fish bites, but we can eliminate as many variables as possible to put the odds in our favor so we can get a hook in them. As an old timer once said, "Ya gotta hook 'em, to cook 'em!" Learning to think like a fish will help at the dinner table.

2

MENU CHOICES

Soft baits come in a wide variety of shapes, sizes and colors to match virtually any species of bait fish you'll need to imitate in your saltwater fishing adventures. There are round ones, skinny ones, long and short, curly tailed and straight, big and small, and some are perfect imitations of the real thing, while others are simply weird looking. Some have wild actions, some are gently seductive. All of them, when carefully chosen and rigged correctly, have the ability to catch fish like few other lures ever invented.

When I look back in the pages of my fishing log, no other lure accounts for more entries than soft-plastic lures; an excellent reason why a soft-plastic lure is usually my go-to lure at the start of most every fishing day when I'll be casting or jigging. I also troll soft plastics, add them to bottom fishing rigs and use them as teasers ahead of a plug when surf fishing. I'm certain there are thousands upon thousands (millions?) of fellow saltwater anglers who also rely on soft baits for a big part of their fishing. Whether in Jupiter, Florida or Point Pleasant, New Jersey, tackle shops all along the coast know what their customers want, and most shops have walls of soft-plastic lures on display ready to do battle with local gamefish. Hey, they work!

When selecting soft-plastic lures, be aware that there is considerable overlap in the names that each manufacturer uses to describe its baits. For instance, the Bass Assassin shads look very much like a Lunker City Slug-Go, and one manufacturer's split-tail minnow may look like another's jerk shad. Berkley's Swimming Minnow, Lunker City's HydroTail, Mister Twister's Ribbon Tail and Thunder Worm, Sea Striker's Curltail Grub and the Mann's Draggin Worm are all variations of the same curly-tail worm, but with different names.

Although the manufacturer's names can sometimes fool you, when choosing a soft bait just select the shape that you want regardless of the moniker the manufacturer hangs on it. In upcoming chapters we'll talk in more detail about each of the soft-plastic bait styles, how to rig them and fish them, and what choices you can make to catch more fish with plastics.

For now, let's take a quick look-see at the menu of choices to see the full range of what's available for coastal anglers. The collection is comprehensive and varied, running from traditional baits to some exotic creations.

TRADITIONAL WORMS

The start of the soft-plastic lure craze began with the "rubber" worm and today the worm is still a favorite bait for many saltwater fishermen. They come in many lengths that vary from tiny 3-inch sizes that imitate a clam worm, to jumbo 12-inch versions that look remarkably like a pencil-size eel or a natural sea worm. They also come with straight tails, rounded tails, curly tails and flat tails; and with ribbed or smooth bodies, fat shapes and slender shapes.

Some worms are molded to exactly resemble the flattened, many-legged look of a natural sandworm, and these imitators are considered among the best choices when rigging a fake worm to be drifted toward a bridge piling, fished on the bottom near structure where striped bass are known to hang out, or when slow trolled with a spinner rig.

A favorite worming technique uses a Berkley PowerBait worm rigged with a single hook in its nose, and allowed to drift at night into the shadow line cast from a lighted bridge. If the tide stage is right and the striped bass are in residence, the strikes will be fast and furious.

A falling tide was the perfect time to catch this pair of weakfish that were caught on Fin-S Fish worked along the edge of a drop-off close to a back-bay sandy beach.

Depending on the specific formula the manufacturer uses, plastic worms, can float, sink or have neutral buoyancy; and each quality makes that particular worm the right choice for very specific situations. A floating worm rides high in the water if rigged without a weight and is a great choice when you want to drift and float a worm over a shallow mussel or sand bar to stripers or weakfish waiting for an easy meal to be washed to them in the current. Texas rigged or rigged with a leadhead at the nose, the floating worm rides tail-high for an especially attractive action. A worm-and-bucktail is standard fare for many weakfish sharpies using a 6- to 10-inch worm behind a bucktail to work inlets, drop-offs, underwater shoals and deep holes.

In the salt chuck, the most popular colors include the standard variety of bright attractors like pearl, chartreuse and pink, along with the more subtle and natural-looking dark green, motor oil, purple, red and black. Color choice depends on what you are trying to accomplish; imitate natural-looking bait or offer something bright in cloudy water or deep water.

Color choice sometimes seems to be of no particular importance, yet at times it can be the essential fish-catching factor. One morning, well before the sky began to glow with the promise of the new day, a buddy and I fished side by side, catching school striped bass in the Point Pleasant Canal; he used a pink worm tail, mine was pearl. In the dark, the number of strikes was about even and we went fish for

From Long Island's Peconic Bay to the big Delaware Bay, the plastic-worm-and-lead-head combination is still a favorite traditional way to fool weakfish.

fish until there was enough light to tie a knot without need of a neck light. It was as if a switch had been flipped, his pink worm tail stopped catching and my pearl tail was the hot ticket. After three fish in less than ten minutes and no strikes on his lure, he switched to a pearl tail and hooked another bass after only two or three casts. For some reason known only to striped bass on that particular morning, pearl was the better color in the first light of dawn, but an hour earlier, color didn't seem to matter at all.

The array of worm colors, lengths, styles and variations of shapes is enormous—too much for any angler to lug around in a tackle bag, so it's important to select and carry only what colors and styles will really work in your area. A visit to a local tackle shop is always helpful to determine which worms are in favor. Some freshwater choices can be quickly eliminated, such as worms with bright tails, which make a great target for small bluefish, southern snappers, sheepshead and other short-striking little bait stealers that will ruin worm after worm. You also don't need 10 variations of blue, purple, black and deep red; pick just a few and stick with the basics. As an example, I've had good luck with the Bass Assassin curly-tail worms, but they make over two dozen variations of the four basic dark colors. I can't possibly carry them all so I just choose one variation of each and stick with those basic colors.

In upcoming chapters we'll talk about how to rig plastic worms for deep jigging, trolling, inshore and back-bay casting, surf and jetty casting, bottom fishing and drift fishing; for now let's just say that soft-plastic worms are a very effective bait and you'll want to have some in your lure arsenal.

TUBE BAITS

Here's another freshwater creation that has begun to enjoy amazing success in saltwater. With their hollow bodies and tentacle-like skirts at the tail end, tube baits look just like a natural squid, so it's no wonder they catch fish in the brine. Like all plastic baits they come in a huge selection of color combinations, and there is a tube-bait size to fool everything from saltwater panfish like snappers, pompano and winter flounder, to hefty yellowfin tuna, jumbo striped bass, tiderunner weakfish and 'gator-size trout.

They can be rigged weightless on Z-hooks, Texas or Carolina style with nose weights or draped onto a standard leadhead. Hook manufacturers have also devised several special set ups that place small weights that are attached to the hook inside the hollow body like Owner's Phantom hook system. They are great for fishing shallow-water areas over grass beds, sandy shoals and mussel bars. One of my

Hollow tube baits are one of the liveliest-looking soft baits, and they can be fished on a leadhead, a worm hook or special Phantom hooks for optimum action.

favorite techniques for tube baits is to fish them vertically around bridge and dock pilings or on the edge of steep drop-offs at channels or deep holes. There are also specially shaped leadheads that slip entirely inside the body of the tube bait for a realistic looking lure that has plenty of mass and weight to fish deep water.

As with other soft baits the color selection seems to be limitless and they are available in short 2-inch sizes suitable for winter flounder and croaker rigs, to mega sizes of 6 to 8 inches in length and over an inch in diameter that can be used to fool near-shore striped bass and offshore tuna and dolphin.

Because the bodies of tube baits are hollow many guides like to stuff cotton or Styrofoam packing peanuts inside the body, soaking the cotton or packing material with fish oil, gel or paste for added scent attraction.

JERKBAITS

Herb Reed of Lunker City Lures is generally credited with popularizing and developing the soft-plastic jerkbait craze in the Northeast with his famous Fin-S Fish and Slug-Go family of baits, but jerkbaits have enjoyed amazing success from Maine to Texas. Along the Texas Gulf Coast from Galveston through Matagorda Island, Corpus Christi and the vast Laguna Madre estuary, the Bass Assassin in strawberry red with silver glitter, the avocado with red glitter and the coppery color called new penny were the hot lures for many years, and still catch plenty of trout and reds today. Other popular colors included the purple and chartreuse combination and a fluorescent glow bait with a chartreuse tail.

Another hot soft bait that has been catching trout and reds since the 1960s is the Kelly Wiggler with its long body and "shrimpy" silhouette. After 40 years of success, this soft bait is still considered to be a must-have lure for Texas inshore anglers.

Nearby off the Louisiana Coast, the Cocahoe Minnow enjoys a long history and well-deserved reputation as a proven fish catcher. Fishing the Cocahoe is simply a way of life for local Cajuns—same as shrimp Creole, crawfish gumbo, chickory coffee and sugary beignets.

In the Northeast and mid-Atlantic, the bubblegum Fin-S Fish put jerkbaits on the map for saltwater fishermen. I had fished Fin-S Fish tails slid onto leadheads for many years for school stripers and especially for tiderunner weakfish, and knew of the lure's fish-catching powers, and had also fished Slug-Go baits in the same manner; but Jim White of White Ghost Charters in Rhode Island, showed me how effective they were when rigged weightless and cast on light plugging tackle. His enthusiasm for the lure was obvious as he showed me how he rigged it to run just below the surface to fool striped bass with amazing side-to-side action.

Jerkbaits are a favorite soft-plastic offering all along the coast. This redfish couldn't resist a jerkbait fished on a small leadhead and retrieved across a shallow grass flat.

"The weight of the lure and the hook are just enough to cast well on light conventional tackle, and the jerky, sweeping retrieve makes the lure dance like crazy," he told me, and with that he whipped off a cast that sent a pearl 6-inch Slug-Go into the waters of a quiet cove off Narragansett Bay. A few moments later, just as Jim predicted, a 15-pound bass swiped the lure; proof positive that this was a lure I had to try back home. Jim uses Fin-S Fish and Slug-Go lures on virtually a daily basis in his light-tackle guiding in his home waters in Rhode Island, and you know the reason—they work.

Called jerkbaits because they are designed to be retrieved with jerks of the rod tip, these soft-plastic creations have an amazing side-to-side, cork screw twisting, sweeping, darting action that drives many saltwater gamefish absolutely nuts—they just can't resist taking a swipe at them. Well-known writer and coastal angler, Bob McNally, told me that he fishes jerkbaits for everything from redfish to stripers and trout and says it's one of his most productive soft lures. "In shallow water, jerkbaits are a great way to fool fish. I use them all the time."

Most coastal anglers are more familiar with jerkbaits, also called split-tail minnows, as a soft-tail bait pushed onto the shank of a bucktail or leadhead. Fished with a hopping retrieve, the slender tails add color and motion and enjoy a terrific reputation for their fish-catching prowess. Along the Northeast and mid-Atlantic stretches of the coast, they are "go-to" lures for catching weakfish and sea trout, and like the credit card ad says, local anglers "don't leave home without it." A good supply of jerkbaits in their tackle bags is essential to a good day's fishing. Bubble gum pink, chartreuse and brown are popular colors, as is the rainbow trout coloration with its green back, pink sides and silver belly.

Jumbo-size jerkbaits like the huge 9-inch Fin-S Fish, 10-inch Slug-Go, and the big YUM Houdini Shad and YUM Forked Tail Dinger are finding a dedicated following in the surf where they are fished near the surface and have nearly replaced live eels as the go-to bait for many sharpies plying the edge of the surf. D. J. Muller, surf guru and author of *The Surfcaster's Guide to the Striper Coast*, is absolutely sold on them. "I began using the big Slug-Go baits after spending some valuable time with Steve McKenna of Rhode Island, who graciously showed me the right way to rig them. Steve is the master at Slug-Go fishing for big striped bass, and I wanted to learn from the best. Thanks to lessons from Steve, I've caught bass in Jersey and New England on these amazing baits." As more surf and jetty fishermen learn about these big, soft baits, they will only continue to become more popular. Make no mistake; they are deadly on striped bass.

At the other extreme, small 2- and 3-inch jerkbaits also make great teasers for surfcasting and inshore coastal casting. Rig them on short leaders about 12 to 18 inches ahead of the main lure and your strikes will definitely increase. Noted surfcasting authority Milt Rosko says, "I've been a big fan of surf teasers for many years because they attract more strikes whenever I fish the surf. They get results and it's a rare day that I don't have a soft-plastic teaser tied above my main lure."

THE SHRIMP FAMILY

You know the old joke, "It's a dirty job, but someone has to do it." Mark Nichols did all the dirty work to develop the perfect artificial shrimp, and for several years he experimented and fished with many, many prototypes before settling on what was to become his innovative, trend-setting lure—the D.O.A. Shrimp. How good is it? Well, many of the top professional guides won't leave the dock without a supply of fake shrimp in their lure bags and it's the lure they recommend their customers stock up on before stepping on the boat. Along the Gulf Coast and Florida, the D.O.A. Shrimp has become the favorite lure of guides, pros and local sharpies.

This snook ate an artificial shrimp cast up tight to a mangrove edge. It's about to be released to assure good fishing tomorrow.

I've been blessed with opportunities to fish with several of the best Florida guides who rely on D.O.A. Shrimp to earn their daily bread, and have seen first-hand how they catch fish with amazing success. If they didn't catch, the guides wouldn't take up space on the boat, so you know they have to be good.

Shrimp now come in a wide collection of standard and jointed styles in many, many colors and sizes from several manufacturers. Some are sold as un-rigged baits meant to be rigged by the angler on a jig head, others pre-rigged and ready to fish. They all look very realistic and their popularity is rising—even up north on the coast where there is still some reluctance to try them. They can be fished Texas- and Carolina-style, as a drop-shot rig or on a three-way rig.

CLAMS, CRABS, SQUID AND MORE

Hey, if fake shrimp work well, why not fake crabs? Well, they do. So do soft-plastic imitations of sand fleas. Berkley Gulp! is even packaged in a special clam-bait shape, kind of a blob, but with plenty of scent to fool fish.

Squid have been popular in the salt for many years, primarily used as daisy chains for offshore species of gamefish, like tuna and marlin, but they also have become standard fare for inshore work when bottom fishing for summer flounder. The small squid adds color, mass and silhouette to the presentation and can sometimes account for many more strikes. Squids can also be slipped onto a leadhead and cast to inshore stripers or dolphin around buoys or weed lines.

Squid colors are usually limited to the basic natural, pink, lime, dark brown, amber, purple and red, but for most situations that's sufficient. Sizes range from 1½-inch miniatures to jumbo 12- to 14-inch monsters meant to fool big tuna, swordfish or marlin.

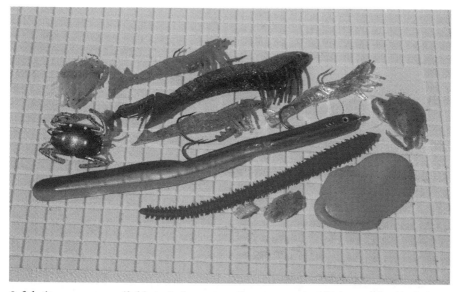

Soft baits are now available to imitate virtually every natural bait possible—including clams! This collection also includes sand fleas, worms, shrimp, crabs and eels.

Also in the lineup of potential soft baits are some weird shapes that freshwater fishermen use to imitate crawdads or crayfish, which are dead ringers for "baby" lobsters. Some weird shapes like Berkley's Sabretail and the Mann's Draggin Fly are excellent choices for coastal fishing, even though they don't resemble anything in particular in the marine environment. They probably catch fish because they offer an enticing fluttering motion that looks alive and struggling, and this triggers strikes. They are worth a try.

SWIMBAITS
Stripers, school tuna, fluke, dolphin, snook, speckled trout and weakfish all have one thing in common—they love to eat swimbaits! In case you just left a hermit's shack in the mountains, swimbaits are the latest rage for surf, bay, inshore and offshore fishing. Made of soft plastic, these lifelike clones look just like the "real thing, baby," and because of their realism, they are extremely versatile and can be cast in the surf, trolled along the edge of weed line, jigged on the edge of a deep channel or cast to bridge pilings. A swimbait will work virtually everywhere you find gamefish—deep or shallow, day or night, all season long. Depending upon the body shape, swimbaits imitate peanut bunker, mullet, killies, pinfish, shrimp, sand eels and spearing.

What makes them different? It's all in the molding process. A traditional leadhead places the soft plastic tail at the rear of the lure, but swimbaits go one step further. They encase the entire leadhead in soft plastic. This allows the lure designers to develop some unique and extremely lifelike shapes that exactly imitate a variety of natural baits.

One of the earliest swimbait-style lures was the D.O.A. Bait Buster introduced in 1991, but swimbaits really took off with the introduction of the Storm Lures WildEye Swimbait Shad in the mid 1990s. This lure is generally credited with popularizing the swim-bait craze, and as anglers quickly began catching fish like crazy on swimbaits, within a short time, many more manufacturers were on the bandwagon.

This opened up a terrific opportunity for fishermen as the variety of shapes, colors, actions and sizes expanded dramatically. Today, swimbaits are marketed in sizes that range from the tiny to the titanic. For example, Tsunami's selection runs the gamut from their diminutive 2-inch mini shads for panfish and school-size gamefish to their gigantic 9-inch swim shad meant for trophy stripers, cod, amberjack and offshore tuna.

The range of color options is enhanced with the placement of special holographic tapes and foils inside the molded soft plastic, and the

Swimbaits are available from a wide range of lure manufacturers and in many sizes and profiles to imitate slim sand eels and peanut bunker, like this selection from Tsunami.

careful use of plastic dyes and spray-on color schemes. This combination of internal and external coloration allows manufacturers to imitate every nuance of color found in natural baits. Swimbaits can be colored to look lively enough to wiggle out of your hand, slip into the water and swim away. Bright colors, such as pink, chartreuse and pearl are also created to increase a swimbait's visibility in dark or cloudy water. Dark colors, such as root beer, purple, deep red and black, are also favorites in low-light conditions.

From a fishing perspective, one of the most interesting attributes of bucktails, leadheads and swimbaits is the shape and balance of the leadhead itself. The molding process that places the lead inside the soft-plastic body, also allows the shape of the lead to be configured in new ways that produce unique retrieve actions. The weight can be shaped long or short, or placed centered on the hook shank or below it. Typical positions include placing the weight along the lower portion of the lure, at the front, or stretched out through a longer portion of the body. Each design option provides a different retrieve action and adds an extra measure of fishability to the swimbait family of lures.

Swimbaits have been created in a wide variety of body shapes that include long and slender, and short and fat. The goal is to match the local baitfish in profile and size. The side profile is only one aspect of swimbait shape. When looked at head on, swimbaits can have a wide, rounded head shape, or a slender, thin-face shape. This is important, because the width of the lure will alter the swimbait's swimming characteristics. Slender shapes generally fish better in very shallow water with a hopping, twitching retrieve, while fat body shapes tend to fish best in deeper water.

BALLYHOO AND BUNKER BAITS

Mann's Baits, Mold Craft Lures and Williamson Lures offer some amazingly lifelike reproductions of ballyhoo that are easy to rig, very tough and nearly as effective as a fresh-dead bally. Chuck Richardson's Tournament Cable company offers pre-rigged soft-plastic ballyhoo manufactured by Calcutta Baits that are used by many offshore anglers with great success.

Offshore crews would usually prefer to fish with a fresh ballyhoo, but there are times when the bait supply runs low and a fake bally may be just the right choice to get a hook into one or two more sailfish or dolphin. Artificial ballyhoo can be rigged quickly, and are especially easy to rig on a circle hook; this is the hot conservation thing to do for many billfish anglers and captains.

Artificial ballyhoo, cigar minnows, mackerel-type baits and squids can also be rigged on dredges, giant underwater teasers that imitate a ball of bait to attract the interest of sailfish. The artificials have a distinct advantage over natural baits because they can be used over and over again, since they need no refrigeration, only clean storage in between fishing trips. They can be repaired easily to keep a dredge operational, another advantage that offshore crews really appreciate. Natural baits have to be prepared and re-rigged on every trip, costing valuable time and added expense.

Mann's offers a giant soft-plastic Mannhaden, which is the spitting image of a natural menhaden (bunker) bait. It has been very effective as the drop-back teaser on umbrella rigs when trolling for striped bass, and is quite capable of fooling yellowfin tuna when slipped onto the hook of an 8-ounce leadhead and dropped to the deep.

An important soft-plastic bait for Northeast surf and jetty casters are the eel imitations marketed by Berkley, Crème and DeLong. They are rigged with leadheads for casting as a replacement for natural old-time favorite rigged eel, and they can also be rigged for surf-casting in place of a live eel. Southern fishermen have used imitation eels to cast to cobia and offshore they make a great white marlin trolling bait.

Williamson Lures has taken the realistic soft-bait one step beyond and markets lifelike bonito, skipjack, mackerel and cutlass fish (rib-

For inshore and offshore fishing, new additions to the life-like lineup of soft-plastic lures include perfect imitations of ballyhoo, cutlass fish and mackerel.

bonfish) that are gaining in popularity with the blue-water fraternity. They are factory rigged to be well balanced and with paddle tails for amazing swimming actions.

Several companies now have interesting hybrid lures like the Mann's Sea Snake, a 19-inch deep swimmer with a Stretch 30+ body and a soft-plastic tail. In the water the lure looks awesome and has become a striped bass favorite.

With patience to rig them properly, anything is possible, inshore or offshore, with big soft baits.

SOFT-BAIT CARE AND "FEEDING"

Because of their chemical make-up, care must be exercised when storing soft-plastic baits, but thankfully there are many easy solutions that will keep your lures safe and cozy, and ready for fishing. The softening chemicals in plastic baits will attack some hard plastics and some paint finishes—that means hard-plastic lures, painted bucktails, painted jigs and some storage boxes are open to "attack" and will literally melt when touched by a soft bait.

Most tackle boxes and storage bags are soft-plastic friendly so you don't have to worry too much, but it's always a good idea to test a new storage container first. As an example, a new surf bag I purchased recently had plastic insert tubes to hold poppers, swimming plugs and needlefish lures. I slipped a large soft-plastic shad into one of the tubes and when I opened the bag two days later for my next surf session, the shad had melted to the plastic insert tube effectively welding itself to the side of the tube. A poor choice of material by the manufacturer and laziness on my part to check whether the tubes were plastic-friendly turned out to be a bad combination.

When asked to share the same storage box, container or bag, soft baits will usually bleed their individual colors into one another, eventually causing a mixed bag of chartreuse, pink, gold, purple and white to morph into a beautiful (huh?) shade of brownish mush. Colors must be kept separated to retain their color integrity.

Sunlight can also ruin the color integrity of soft baits. A bag of chartreuse shad tails I once left on the console of my boat for several hours became totally clear with no color at all after basking in the sun's UV rays. Luckily the embedded silver flecks still gave the lures plenty of flash so they continued to catch fish, but there wasn't a trace of chartreuse left in them. Keep your plastics out of the sun in a tackle bag, storage compartment in your boat or beach buggy, or even tucked away in your pocket if you are wade fishing.

It must be a natural, in-born trait of fishermen to bring along enough tackle, lures and gear for every conceivable fishing possibility, and with soft baits there's the tendency to want to bring along every possible color, size and shape, plus an inventory of jig heads and hooks. Charter skippers and guides cringe when customers show up with armloads of tackle boxes and lure bags filled with everything but the kitchen sink.

So how do we store and then carry all this stuff without breaking our backs? The first step is the basic flat, multi-compartment utility tackle tray. Is there a fisherman anywhere who doesn't use utility trays? Impossible, I'd bet. They're made in many sizes with slip-in partitions so they convert into almost any storage configuration needed, and they form the basis of tackle storage systems in hard and soft-plastic tackle boxes, in built-in storage compartments designed for boats and beach buggies, and they can be stacked in a workshop area to hold everything from hooks and jig heads to all types of plastic tails. In my home workshop, I keep individual boxes stored above my workbench for worms, shads, curly tails, shrimp, jerkbaits, leadheads, hooks and rigging supplies. Everything is handy to reach, with great visibility to see what's inside each box.

Industrial-grade, clear-plastic parts bags are available in an infinite variety of sizes. Their zip-type closures keep out saltwater, keep lure colors separated and are small enough to fit nicely into your shirt pocket, jetty bag or the pouch inside the front of your waders.

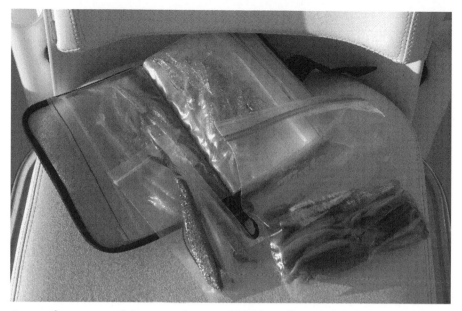

Among the many good storage options are foldable wallet-style lure holders and zip-type bags in several sizes. Store the zip bags in a tackle drawer, tackle bag or water-proof plastic-lid container.

Usually sold in bulk quantities, it's a good idea to team up with a buddy or two, or a fishing club, to place an order, which can be split up among several fishermen. I use the 3- by 6-inch size and order them from U-Line Company (www.uline.com).

Ventilated mesh bags are another good choice, especially for larger soft baits and offshore lures such as squid daisy chains or giant leadheads with jumbo-size plastic tails. They are sold in one-, three- and five-compartment configurations, and while designed primarily to hold offshore lures, they do double duty on the inshore grounds, too. The vented back allows quick drying, while the clear front panel lets you see what's inside each bag for quick access.

A walk down the aisle of any supermarket will net you some handy tackle storage items not usually sold in tackle shops. Zipper-type plastic bags come in many shapes and sizes to hold bulk quantities of soft-plastic tails. I store the bags in water-proof plastic containers. These tough boxes take a lot of knocking around. An added advantage; squirt fish oil into the bag, drop a few soft tails into it, then seal the bag for tomorrow's fishing session.

Recycled peanut butter jars offer similar storage options for holding large quantities of a soft-tail lure or tails of a large size, and to store extra leadheads. In summer when the striped bass fishing gets tough because of the soft-plastic eating bluefish that invade some of my favorite haunts, I need to carry a good supply of tails to replace the repeated cut-offs. The small peanut butter jars are very handy.

Fly fishing leader wallets and freshwater worm wraps are handy for storing a variety of saltwater-size soft-plastic lures. I use a fly leader wallet for storing fluke, flounder, sea bass and bottom rigs, pre-rigged with soft tails. A Tackle Logic Worm Wrap has zip closure bags and was initially designed to hold freshwater worms. It works just great for saltwater soft plastics, like jerkbaits, squids, shrimp, shads and curly tails.

With so much to choose from, tackle storage is easier today than ever before. The choice of materials enhances durability of the storage system, and the flexibility designed into many of them allows the same bag to be used for many types of fishing, simply by interchanging the utility trays. If you're a pack rat, the choices are wide open, and they take up less space.

Soft tackle bags are the most flexible way to carry a lot of soft baits. The L.L. Bean canvas bag is the simplest soft tackle "garage" and it's been doing yeoman duty for over 50 years. The zippered top is handy to keep salt spray away, and their shape is hard to beat for stuffing foul weather gear, thermos, boots, camera and lunch into a handy package. A soaking in saltwater is quickly fixed with a rinse

Having the right lure ready at the right time will get you hooked up in no time. Linda Barrett cast a soft-plastic lure to surface-crashing crevalle jacks and hooked a big one just off Lake Worth Inlet.

from the garden hose, or run the bag through the washing machine for a thorough end-of-season cleaning. The medium L.L. Bean bag holds up to four 3700-size or a half dozen 3600-size utility boxes—that's a huge amount of storage capacity in a relatively small bag.

Backpacks, like the type students use to carry their textbooks, are also terrific for lugging a small amount of tackle for a day's fishing. A small bag can hold up to three utility trays, a jig or bucktail punch, tools and sunscreen. The soft, flexible sides allow the pack to fit into a storage compartment on any boat, and they are relatively waterproof. A quick spray with Scotchguard will help shed water as the pack gets worn. Because metal zippers corrode, look for a pack with vinyl zippers to avoid the ravages of saltwater.

For even more storage, Plano and Flambeau offer special stackable "tackle stations," designed like backpacks and built from the get-go to hold tons of tackle, lures and gear. The largest tackle stations hold up to eight utility boxes for maximum versatility. Light-tackle anglers like small backpacks or jetty bags, especially for wading, or when fishing with a guide in a small boat. I've been using a Shimano Baltica bag for lugging around my inshore and bay tackle and have been real pleased with the bag's versatility. Five 3600-size utility trays slip into the main compartment. They hold my leadheads and soft plastic tails and swimbaits, and an assortment of hooks, sinkers, rigs, leaders and floats. The side pockets hold pliers, hook-outs, flashlight, sun screen lotion, bug spray, leader wheels, a jug of water and more.

A great bag when you are fishing with a guide is the Able Trout bag (Steve Able probably meant rainbow trout, but he could have meant coastal sea trout—anyway it's a great shallow water bag). It's padded so it floats if it takes a dive overboard, it holds up to three 3600-size utility trays and it has numerous compartments to hold pocket camera, hooks, weights, line scissors, leader wallet, sun screen, sunglasses and a lot more. It's misnamed, but a terrific bag.

ADD-ONS

Fishermen like to tinker with lures, always with an eye to make them better fish catchers, and with soft plastics there are several options to customize and tune up lures for better casting performance for you and enhanced visual appeal to the fish.

Many anglers believe gamefish home-in on the eye of a baitfish. In nature, there are numerous examples of forage fish with large spots on their tails to confuse predators, and these fish evolved over millions of years. If investing that much time and evolutionary effort to avoid capture is so important, then it sure can't hurt to make sure your lures have eyes on them.

Some lures, of course, are manufactured with eyes already in place, but many plastic tails have no eyes at all. It's easy to add an eye with the stick-on eyes sold in every fly fishing shop, some specialty tackle shops and through mail order outlets. Stick-on eyes are available on flat reflective tape cut into circles from ⅛ inch to ¼ inch or more in diameter, as are 3-D doll eyes, which have the added advantage of sound as the pupils rattle inside the round chamber. One word of caution, fresh, new tails have a slimy surface residue that must be wiped clean to help the eye stick in place. A quick wipe with a boat towel will usually do the trick. A dab of CA glue will also help keep the eye in place.

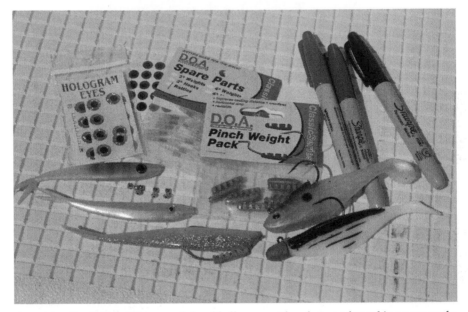

A variety of weights, stick-on and dumbbell eyes, rattles, dyes, and marking pens make it easy to customize lures in a matter of seconds.

To add weight and an eye, use the dumbbell-shaped eyes sold in fly fishing shops to make the famous Clouser Minnow fly pattern, or a section of bead chain, like the kind used as a pull chain on a ceiling fan or desk light. I use an American Littoral Society tagging needle to poke a small hole through the bait, then push the eye into place.

Slender lead weights are another excellent way to add weight to a soft bait. Lunker City and D.O.A. offer small-diameter nail weights that slip inside a shrimp, Slug-Go or Fin-S Fish, worm, shad or jerkbait to add nose or tail weight, or to balance a lure so it swims with a unique action.

Pinch-on weights that crimp to the shank of a Z-hook are a great way to add weight when rigging jerkbaits, shrimp, worms, tube baits and shads. Pinch-on weights are found at tackle shops that specialize in freshwater bass fishing, in mail order catalogs such as Cabela's and Bass Pro and from D.O.A. Lures.

Another excellent soft-lure insert is a rattle chamber. I've been using chambers marketed by Bass Pro and D.O.A. Lures for many years and am a firm believer that a rattling, ticking, clicking sound can improve the potential of many lures to catch fish. The chambers are so small that they can easily be pushed inside a worm, shrimp, shad—virtually any soft-plastic bait—without destroying the shape or balance of the lure.

Color can be added in several ways. One of the easiest is with a permanent-ink marking pen. A pearl or white plastic tail or worm can be quickly changed to a lure with a green, black, blue or red back with two swipes of a marking pen. Be aware that the ink may not quickly dry and may come off on your fingers and on the boat if you're not careful. Marking pens allow the angler to quickly change the tail and head color of a soft lure, or add vertical and horizontal stripes.

Pre-packaged waterproof dyes are also available at tackle shops and mail order suppliers, and with a quick dip, any plastic bait can be altered. Most common is a dip of the tail to add some flash or a contrasting color for gamefish to home-in on, but heads can be dipped, and the entire bait, too. Be careful, most dyes take a second or two to dry and you don't want this stuff dripping on your boat deck—unless you want a chartreuse, pink and purple-spotted deck! The dyes seem to work best when a dark dye is imposed on a light-color plastic tail, not as well as a light dye on a dark tail.

Ever think of using a soft bait as a surface popper? You can by adding a foam popper head like the kind sold in fly shops, or the D.O.A. Chug Head. Either head can be slipped onto the line before the lure is tied into place, then slid down the line to rest at the nose of the soft bait. Popper heads convert a worm, shad or jerkbait into a mighty fine surface splasher that is an exceptional lure for snook, sea trout and weakfish, striped bass and even redfish.

3

PROVEN RIGS FOR WORMS AND MORE

Each spring along the Northeast and mid-Atlantic coasts, tiderunner weakies and school stripers invade coastal bays followed soon after by tasty and fun-to-catch summer flounder. It's that time of year when many saltwater anglers will be flinging leadheads or bucktails dressed with soft plastic tails in hopes of scoring a good catch of these great game fish. Likewise, in the Southeast and along the Gulf coast, leadheads rigged with plastic tails will be the standard offering for snook, jacks, reds, tarpon and trout.

The usual method to rig saltwater soft plastics, whether you fish north or south, is straight forward and simple—slide a soft tail up the hook of a leadhead or bucktail and cast away. Maybe you'll add a squid strip, fish belly or small piece of shrimp for some smell, or a squirt of bunker or shedder crab oil scent. These time-tested methods work most of the time, but anyone who has seriously, avidly fished the coast will have had days when their favorite gamefish just won't bite on the standard table fare and they need something new to attract their attention.

To be a winner on the tough days, having a few extra tricks up your sleeve will help you catch more fish than your fishing partners who don't (or won't) try new ideas. On most days, the traditional rigs will catch plenty of fish, but when stripers or trout get lockjaw, what do you do? That question has some interesting answers, some of them developed in the world of freshwater fishing.

Savvy coastal saltwater fishermen are beginning to take after their freshwater brethren. No, they're not yelling "Son!" when they hook up to a good fish, but they are becoming familiar with terms and techniques like Texas rig, drop-shotting, Carolina rig, wacky rig and spinner rigs. Although originating with tournament bass fishermen for specific fishing applications such as presenting soft baits in heavy weed and brush cover, vertical fishing along drop-offs or shallow water flats fishing these techniques work just as well for salt-water fishermen seeking summer flounder, striped bass, snook, weakfish and seatrout and redfish. The explosion of redfish tournaments from the Carolinas through Florida and up into the Gulf coasts of Alabama, Mississippi and Louisiana has helped popularize the red-fish craze, and have also been the catalyst for introducing many freshwater techniques into the saltwater world.

Salty inshore fishermen have also invented their own techniques like the surf-rigged Slug-Go baits, and the three-way rig developed by saltwater fishermen to drop soft baits down deep around wrecks and reefs, and in deep inlets and over shoals where striped bass and snook hang out.

Most of these rigs began life as new and better ways to effectively fish the ubiquitous rubber worm, yet it is a huge mistake to think these are only worm-rigging techniques because they are also appropriate in many fishing situations to properly rig a jerkbait, shad body, curly tail, tube bait, shrimp or worm. Summer flounder are suckers for a drop-shot rigged jerkbait or tube bait fished low and near the bottom, the Carolina rig is deadly for shallow-water weakfish and speckled trout, and a spinner rig fished along a rocky shore-line will catch striped bass with amazing success.

It is essential to keep your mind open to all the possibilities available when rigging soft baits for salt-water fishing. These rigs are not just a "worm thing," but can be used for virtually any soft bait and for most any fish you encounter along the coast. The rig you select should match the fishing condi-tions such as deep or shallow water, oyster bar or clear sandy bottom, wide flats or edges of drop-offs; and the style of

Freshwater bass rigs and techniques work just as well for saltwater gamefish like this school-size striped bass that eagerly took a soft-plastic bait.

fishing required to catch the gamefish you are targeting such as deep jigging, slow surface retrieve, bounce the bottom slowly, casting to bridge pilings or slow trolling.

HOOKS AND WEIGHTS

The basic methods of rigging a worm or soft bait will rely on two hook styles; the standard straight-shank J-hook and the bent-shank Z-hook, so called because its profile somewhat resembles the slash of Zorro when viewed from the side. There are also special nose weights unique to this style of soft-bait rigging, and if you're not familiar with the hooks, weights and rigging options, check out what's available at a tackle shop that offers a comprehensive selection of sweetwater hooks and rigging weights for largemouth bass. You'll find that a lot of what the bass'n boys use will work just fine for rigging soft-plastic baits in saltwater.

The hook assortment is extensive, and there's a long list of manufacturers offering high-quality and technologically advanced designs with hook bends and shank bends that help rig a bait for maximum hook-setting ability or to help present the bait in the most lifelike manner. The short-shank J-hook is most often used with wacky rigs, trolling rigs and drop-shot rigs, which we'll check out in the next few pages. Z-hooks are usually used with worms, jerkbaits, tube baits and shrimp. When the point of a Z-hook is embedded into the soft-plastic bait, the lure becomes virtually weedless and snagless. This is a big plus when working the lure over eelgrass beds for weakfish, or over clam beds for stripers. The lures will slide right over rocks or bump off a dock piling or other underwater obstructions that would hang up a lure armed with trebles.

It's best to avoid bronzed freshwater-style hooks because they absolutely will rust in a very short time when fished in the salt chuck. Most manufacturers offer black nickel-plate finishes that hold up just great in the salt environment, and some also offer stainless steel hooks, which are virtually rust and corrosion free, and some hooks are available that are specially coated from the get-go just for the saltwater environment. Hooks marketed with a red finish are also resistant to saltwater corrosion—unless you leave them in a water-soaked pack for a week or two.

For saltwater species, hook sizes from 1/0 to 6/0 are about right for most worms, jerkbaits, tube baits and shrimp. You want to match the size hook to the size of the bait; smaller bait, smaller hook. If you're new to this style of rigging, experiment with only one hook style first, then after you gain confidence try some of the other styles that include a variety of special shapes, colors and

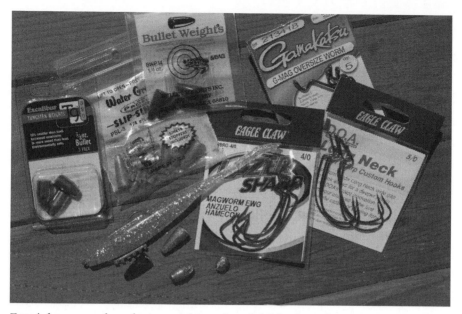

Egg sinkers, cone-shaped nose weights and special Z-hooks make rigging worms, jerk-baits, tube baits and other soft baits an easy job.

unique ways to add weights. Most Z-hooks are sold in packs of 6 to 12 hooks per package so the initial investment in new hooks does not have to be excessive.

Two of the most popular rigs, the Texas rig and the Carolina rig, require a nose weight for the best presentation. Many saltwater fishermen already have a collection of egg sinkers, or leads, on hand that are used to rig live shrimp, trolling ballyhoo or sea worms and in weights of ¼ to ¾ ounce. These traditional leads will work just fine for saltwater versions of the Texas and Carolina worm rigs, however, check out the assortment of tapered nose weights manufactured specifically for worm rigging. Tackle shops sell lead, tungsten and brass weights and they are available in several varieties of the basic cone shape in a wide range of weights. The cone shape has an advantage over the egg sinker because it will slip and glide over bottom obstructions with fewer hang-ups and snags. Nose weights are also available in colors; red, silver, gold, natural lead, white, chartreuse and more, which can add to the rig's attraction.

Some Z-hooks are marketed with a barbed baitholder at the hook eye and a lead weight molded around the hook shank, a handy feature that helps the lure sink when needed and which also acts like a keel guaranteeing that the bait will ride hook-up when retrieved. The D.O.A. Lures pinch-on keel weight is handy because it allows the soft-bait angler to easily add weight, and then remove it, at any time, thereby increasing the bait's versatility.

A few manufacturers also offer Z-hooks with small leadheads, which makes the lure dance much like a traditional bucktail or lead-head, but with the added advantage of being weedless.

Depending on the depth you fish, standard bank sinkers from ½ to 6 ounces will be needed for the many fishing opportunities where a three-way rig is the best choice for inshore bays and deeper fishing over wrecks and reefs. Drop-shot rigs use special weights designed specifically for this fishing technique. A brass or stainless steel eye with a narrow tapered shape captures the line and holds it, allowing the weight to be slid along the line so it can be moved into the optimum position to meet any fishing situation. This is handy, but drop-shotting can also be accomplished in saltwater with standard bank or coin sinkers tied to the end of the line. You lose the ability to slide the sinker into a new position, but this isn't usually important.

Almost every worm or basic plastic bait can be enhanced with rattles, and the addition of stick-on or lead eyes for the extra appeal of sound attraction and a more life-like visual presentation.

BASIC ONE-HOOK RIG

The inherent ability of the soft-plastic bait to semi float on a drift is one of its great virtues. Have you ever watched a sea worm drift in the current? They appear virtually weightless and suspend in the water or sink very slowly while gently twisting and turning seductively. A rubber worm or an imitation sandworm can be rigged on a single hook to duplicate the natural action of a sea worm.

A worm-like bait, large jerkbait or large curly tail bait can be rigged in either of two ways; with no weight in very shallow water, or with a weight to adapt it to fast-running currents or deeper water. You'll add more fish to the cooler with these two basic rigging methods used by local expert anglers and back-bay guides to fool game fish when the usual methods don't pay off. It's a rare weakfish, striper or fluke that will turn up its nose at these lifelike offerings.

The unweighted rig is perfect for casting to fish in water only a foot or two deep, where even a small bucktail or leadhead would have the bait digging into the bottom. The natural unweighted soft bait is still heavy enough to be cast quite well on a light spinning outfit and 6- to 10-pound test mono line, or a light braid of 8- to 15-pound test. When fished with no weight, soft-plastic baits can be fished in very shallow water of only a foot or two deep and will fool striped bass, trout and redfish. If you decide that you need to add weight after the plastic bait is rigged, use a pinch-on lead weight.

This school striped bass couldn't resist a Berkley Gulp! worm drifted toward a bridge abutment in the tidal current.

The keel-weighted hook is ideal for fishing slightly deeper water, and guides like to work it with a twitching action to entice gamefish. Each rigging method offers a different retrieve action so the angler can imitate a wide variety of lifelike bait antics. Baits rigged with weights on the hook shank and positioned along the belly of the plastic bait can be fished in very shallow water and slithered along the bottom much like a sea worm or elver. When twitched slightly on a slow retrieve, they probably look like a live shrimp. They'll go deep if you count a few seconds before starting the retrieve. A slow-paced retrieve is the best speed.

SURF AND INSHORE TEASER RIG

A soft bait rigged on a single hook makes a great teaser when clipped to the main line about 18 inches ahead of the primary lure. A variety of soft baits can be used including the classic Fin-S Fish jerkbait, shads, 4- to 6-inch worms and curly tails. The teaser expands the shapes and profiles, colors and flash that can be presented on every cast. A bright flashy teaser may catch the fish's attention and even if the main lure got bit and hooked the fish, the teaser may have been the deciding factor that caused the strike response.

Many accomplished surfcasters swear by teasers, especially for schoolie striped bass, but they catch jumbo stripers too. Surf-fishing legend Milt Rosko is certain that teasers add dramatically to his catch of striped bass and he rarely fishes in the fall surf without a teaser tied in place. Another surfcasting giant, D. J. Muller, agrees and employs a teaser ahead of swimming plugs, bucktails, swimbaits and larger shads. "The teaser looks like a small bait escaping from a larger bait, and that increases the competitiveness of nearby striped bass. The bass thinks an easy meal is about to get away, and swipes at the teaser."

To make the teaser more durable, use a fly-tying bobbin and wrap a layer of thread around the shank of a J-hook to form an aggressive gripping base to hold the plastic bait firmly in place. Use a bulky thread such as size A or D rod-wrapping thread. Coat the thread wraps with a few drops of super glue to hold them in place and then add a few more drops just before the plastic tail is slipped into place. The extra dab of glue will further increase the durability of the teaser and prevent the tail from slipping down the hook shank each time a short-striking striper tugs at the tail (how do they miss the hook?), and from the force and strain of repeated casting and retrieving.

It's a good idea to make-up teasers ahead of time at a bench in your workshop where you can tie the best knots, make neat thread wraps and accurately measure the leaders, rather than when you are

Surf fishermen often place a small plastic tail on a short leader about 12 to 16 inches ahead of the main lure as a teaser. The visual appearance of a small fish being chased by a big one will trigger plenty of strikes.

fishing and your hands are wet and slippery. Since many surfcasters use a barrel swivel between their main fishing line and the leader, the simplest way to add a teaser to your line is with a Duolock snap. Make up 18-inch fluorocarbon or mono leaders with the hook at one end and the Duolock snap at the other. Simply clip the snap of the teaser leader to the barrel swivel at the top end of the main leader and you are ready to fish. Your pre-made teasers can be handily stored in small zip-type plastic bags like the kind sold in office supply stores measuring 3 by 6 inches, or in a fly fisher's leader wallet.

Short- to medium-length, straight-shank hooks are preferred with no offset at the bend, which causes the teaser to spin. Favorite hook styles include the octopus and beak styles in sizes from size 1 through 2/0. The hook should match the size of the teaser bait and it should not be too heavy to inhibit the teaser's action.

TEXAS RIG

Early plastic worms were rigged with two or three hooks stretched along the length of the worm, sometimes with a spinner ahead of the worm. Conventional wisdom at that time held that a bass would strike a lure from the front, center or rear, and the use of multiple hooks was designed to hook the bass no matter where it struck the bait.

By the end of the 1950s, a new theory emerged, proposing that bass took the lure the same way each time they struck; the fish whacked the lure, turned it and then swallowed the bait. The multiple-hook rigs went the way of the dodo bird and single-hook rigs with the hook positioned at the front of the bait became the most popular way to fish a worm. A nose weight was added to get the lure down to the dining room of the fish.

The new rig had its beginnings with a group of innovative Oklahoma bass fanatics who fished many of the nearby Texas impoundments. The rig became popularized and known as the Texas rig, and "now you know the rest of the story."

The original single-hook worm rigs employed straight-shank Sproat-style J-hooks, but within a short time, this seismic wave of new thinking about worm baits, enhanced by a strong dose of innovation, generated a huge selection of hooks with offset shanks that resembled the Z shape that is so common today, and a wide selection of weight styles.

The Texas rig excels when gamefish are in heavy cover. It is one of the most weedless rigging methods ever devised making it an ideal rig when casting to stripers holding around rocky-bottom areas or to snook in areas with a lot of blow downs, logs and underwater cover. The Texas rig can be worked over oyster bars, shell beds and grass

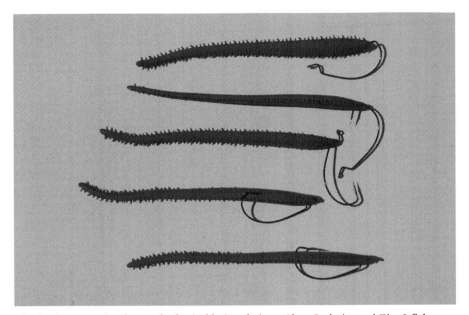

The basic worm rig also works for jerkbaits, shrimp, Slug-Go baits and Fin-S fish. Insert the hook into the nose of the bait about ¼ to ⅜ inch, then push the hook point out the side. Slide the worm down the hook shank toward the eye, and turn it to seat the nose of the worm at the hook eye. Visually check the position of the hook along the side of the worm, then insert the hook into the worm bait. The hook point can be exposed or left inside the bait to make it weedless.

beds without hanging up, and it also works extremely well when casting soft baits around dock pilings or bridges.

To tie the Texas rig, slip a ¼- to ⅜-ounce cone-shaped sinker or a small egg sinker onto the main fishing line and then tie the line directly to the hook with a Palomar or improved clinch knot. Push a toothpick inside the weight, break off what doesn't fit inside the sinker and then slide the sinker down the line until it is positioned at the nose of the worm bait. The toothpick serves as a jam or stopper so the sinker will not slide feely along the line. The stopper is optional, and some anglers prefer a sliding weight. What could be simpler than a Texas rig?

When fishing shallow water with a slow retrieve, a light wire hook is preferred, switching to a larger size heavy-wire hook in deeper water or when fishing a slightly faster retrieve.

A slow to moderate retrieve will usually get more strikes than a fast retrieve, especially in summer when warm water temperatures make some gamefish lethargic and sluggish. An easy lift-drop-pause retrieve makes the worm or plastic bait work like it's alive and gets many strikes. Working the rod tip up and down on the retrieve makes the lure rise and fall with a slow vertical swimming motion that keeps the plastic bait just off the bottom, but within the striking zone of gamefish. The Texas rig when worked with a slow retrieve that slides and bounces the lure along the bottom is an all-time favorite presentation and it can be fished in water from only a foot or two in depth to deep drop-offs.

The Texas rig is a universal rigging method that can be used with jerkbaits, tube baits, worms, eels, shrimp and long-bodied curly-tail baits. It seems to work best with baits that run about 4 to 8 inches in length.

CAROLINA RIG

While the Texas rig ties the leader directly to the hook eye so the lead weight rides right up against the nose of the bait, its close cousin the Carolina rig uses a 12- to 30-inch leader tied between the weight and the soft bait, with a barrel swivel tied between the leader and the main fishing line. An egg sinker or nose weight is slid onto the main fishing line so it rides above the barrel swivel. This allows the Carolina rig to have more motion and the weight also creates a mud

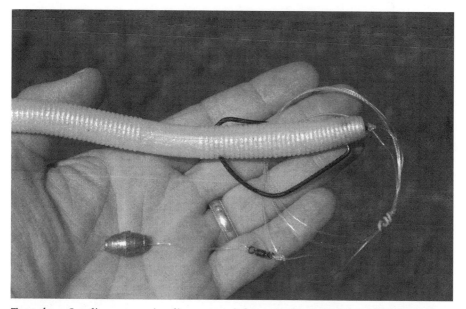

To make a Carolina worm rig, slip an egg sinker onto the main fishing line, then tie on a barrel swivel to trap the sinker above the swivel. Tie a 16- to 24-inch leader to the hook eye and then to the barrel swivel. This rig allows the worm to suspend just above the bottom.

trail or mud puffs when fished on soft bottom. To avoid chafing at the knot, which could eventually cause knot failure, a small plastic bead can be inserted between the egg-sinker and the knot at the barrel swivel. This added protection assures maximum knot strength.

The Carolina rig originated in South Carolina for freshwater bass fishing, but it's a very effective method for fishing in saltwater. With its sinker positioned ahead of the lure, it makes a better vertical presentation and can be cast and retrieved, or jigged vertically. It can be deadly when drifting for fluke, or when weakfish, striped bass, sea trout and croaker are holding in 5 to 14 feet of water along a channel edge. Jig the bait with slight twitches of the rod tip so the lure zips upward a foot then flutters and slides back down.

Sound is easily added to the Carolina rig by adding a glass or plastic bead ahead of the barrel swivel and between the main fishing line and the leader. By working the rod tip so the bait dances up and down, the sinker will make a clicking sound as it moves back and forth on the line and "bangs" against the plastic bead and the barrel swivel. For maximum sound, use a hard metal weight such as brass or stainless steel. They make a sharper, more audible click as compared to the softer lead weights that make more of a thumping sound.

The basic Carolina rig can be modified to make it an even more productive rig in saltwater by replacing the tapered weight or egg-sinker weight with either a bucktail or a plain leadhead with a plastic tail slipped onto the hook. This rig looks somewhat like a backwards surf teaser rig, but because the weight of the leadhead controls the depth of the rig, the appearance of this rig is much different to the fish. The color of the lead-head soft bait can match the same color of the trailing bait at the end of the Carolina rig or it can serve as an attractor of a different color to enhance the visual appeal of the rig. If the primary bait has a natural hue to it, a leadhead with a bright pink or chartreuse tail will make the rig more visible, especially in murky or cloudy water.

This rig is bottom bounced in the same way as the basic Carolina rig relying on lifts of the rod tip to make the leadhead and the primary bait sweep up from the bottom and then slowly settle back down. This technique is especially deadly while drifting along a drop-off, across a bar or when working the rig away from shoreline structure such as a marsh sedge or a mangrove tangle.

Repeated 1- to 2-foot lifts and drops with the rod tip will usually get strikes from the Carolina rig, although a straight-in retrieve with gentle rod lifts can also prove to be very effective at times.

Carolina rigs can be made up at home in your workshop and stored in resealable bags to save rigging time when you're on the water. This requires that you coil the leaders so they fit into the bag.

To be sure the lure works right, stretch the leader before you make the first cast. Another great way to store Carolina rigs employs a 12-inch length of tubular foam, like the kind sold at the hardware store to insulate water pipes, with several rubber bands slipped in place about 2 inches apart. Insert the hook into the foam, wrap the leader around it and then slip the barrel swivel end of the leader under a rubber band. Voila! Easy leader storage.

SINGLE-HOOK JERKBAITS

One of the most popular saltwater soft plastics is the jerkbait; those long slender, slim-profile baits that resemble sand eels, worms, anchovies, glass minnows and elvers. Some jerkbaits are now available with a fatter profile to imitate small herring, peanut bunker and snapper blues.

They got their name from the jerky retrieve method that makes these unique baits dance in a wide, side-to-side sweeping action. This irregular darting action looks so dramatic that many gamefish have a very hard time resisting the chance to strike.

Jerkbaits, like the famous Fin-S Fish, are fished in a variety of ways. In small sizes they must have weight added to be cast, but a 4- to 9-inch jerkbait has enough weight all on its own that it can be cast on light spinning and plugging gear with relative ease. If a small

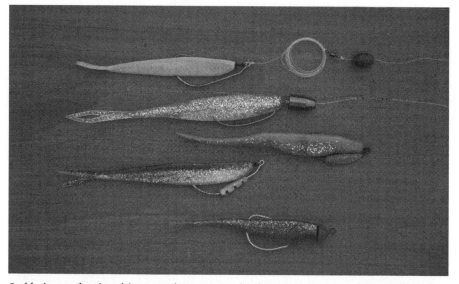

Jerkbaits can be rigged in several ways to make them run deep, suspend at mid-depths or run very shallow. This versatility makes them a great bait for southern and northern gamefish.

amount of weight is needed, nail-like weights are slipped inside the forward portion of the body to help gain casting distance or to get the bait below the surface water. When retrieved with twitches of the rod tip, then a short pause, the jerkbait is a wild lure for striped bass and snook. One change in rigging is suggested; select a Z-hook with a straight shank or with minimal offset so the bait will swim correctly, and rig it so the hook protrudes a small fraction of an inch out of the soft body.

Texas and Carolina rigs, as described above, are also good rigging choices for jerkbaits, and they are then fished much the same manner as a worm bait. Their "jerky" action adds a new dimension of action that cannot be duplicated with a standard worm bait. To save on-the-water rigging time, I like to make up a selection of pre-rigged jerkbait Carolina rigs in various colors and store them in plastic bags. A short 18-inch leader has a Krok barrel swivel at one end and hook eye at the other end. The rig can quickly be tied to the end of the main leader or fishing line in seconds. The egg sinker or nose weight is slipped onto the leader before tying on the jerkbait. The added hardware of the barrel swivel makes this rig slightly less stealthy but speeds up your ability to switch lures if there's a hot striper bite and a leader gets chafed by bass or ripped from bluefish bites. Of course, if you need minimum visibility, do away with the barrel swivel.

DROP-SHOT AND THREE-WAY RIGS

The drop-shot and three-way rigs are excellent choices for straight-up-and-down vertical fishing because they allow the bait to move almost horizontally in the water, exactly imitating how a natural live bait would appear.

Drop-shotting is a technique saltwater fishermen "borrowed" from the freshwater bass pros and it works splendidly when using relatively light plugging tackle in bay and inshore waters of 10 to 20 feet for summer flounder, weakfish and sea trout and school stripers. Bigger fish and deeper water are more effectively fished with the three-way rig in waters up to 60 or more feet of depth. I've fished the three-way rig in 90 feet of water for bottom-hugging striped bass off the Jersey coast and have caught big snapper and grouper off Florida reefs with the same technique.

Both methods place a sinker below the soft bait, suspending the bait at a calculated position off the bottom structure. Depending on the drop-down to the sinker the bait may be positioned anywhere from a few inches off the bottom to several feet. The three-way and drop-shot rigs are at their fish-catching best when gamefish are

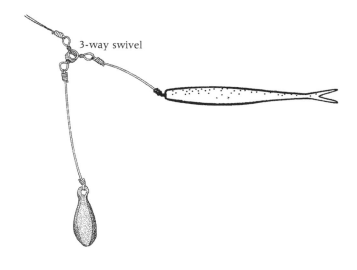

3-way swivel

Three-way rig

tightly schooled over clearly defined structure, such as striped bass or snook in an inlet, over an inshore lump, rock ledge or drop-off, or in a bay area along a channel drop-off, oyster bar, along an inlet sea wall or when drifting around dock pilings.

Because it is fished in relatively shallow water, the drop-shot rig is usually fished while drifting but it can also be worked from an anchored boat in tight areas that are known to hold fish. It's a great match-up with a light spinning or conventional rod-and-reel outfit. The lure action is varied; work the rod tip with a gentle up-and-down motion to imitate a dying baitfish or an injured bait; or with short, rapid lifts and jiggles to make the bait vibrate and dance.

The three-way is a very effective drift rig when fishing for striped bass when they congregate in schools near the bottom on structure like open-bottom shoals in the fall. The three-way can drop a soft-plastic right into the dining room of big bass and a lift-and-drop rod action will usually get jolting strikes.

The freshwater-based drop-shot technique uses special weights manufactured just for this style of fishing, and they can be adapted to saltwater fishing. The brass or stainless-steel weights have unique tightly tapered eyes so as to trap and grip the line firmly. The leader can be loosened from the eye's grip to be slid into a higher or lower position for quick adjustments. If you are worried about losing the weight, tie an overhand knot in the line or leader below the sinker so it won't slip off.

WACKY RIGS

Wacky wormin' has been used by bass pros since the 1980s but is just now becoming popular in saltwater. When you need a technique to present a soft bait while drifting along the edge of a dock piling, a bridge abutment, a marsh sedge or close to mangrove tangle, the wacky rig can do the job very nicely. Snook and striped bass addicts fishing lighted dock pilings on the night shift can fool good numbers of fish with this technique.

Why is it called a wacky rig? Well, it just looks wacky with the hook placed in the center of the bait so the worm ends flop on either side of the hook. At first glance, many a saltwater angler has said, "This thing will never work," but chuck it up against a bridge piling and let it sink down and you'll be pleasantly surprised with bites from stripers, snook, sea bass, and snapper, and in shallow water with strikes from summer flounder. Wacky rigs work best when the currents are not flowing at their peak, or when the boat is drifting at the same speed as the current so the bait can settle in the water and not be swept away.

Casting wacky-rigged bait toward the pilings of a lighted dock is a favorite technique for night-time snook fishing, and also around bridges. A bait can be wacky-rigged on the three-way rig described in the previous section so when the bait is dropped down and then

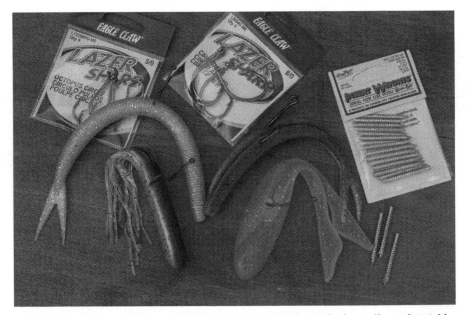

With the hook placed in the middle of the bait, the wacky rig looks, well, wacky! Add a nail weight to one end to make the bait flutter more, and jig with short twitches of the rod tip.

gently jigged by moving the rod tip, it gets the fish's attention. This is an effective way to catch sea bass, grouper and snapper and striped bass in deep water, or to fool trout and weakfish along channel edges.

Like all these basic "worm" rigs, the wacky rig can be used with almost any soft bait; worms, jerkbaits, tube baits and Slug-Gos, and they can be fished with or without weight, below a float or all alone. The best weights are the nail-like weights marketed by Lunker City pushed into one end, or both ends, of the bait. With a nail pushed into one end, the bait tends to corkscrew towards the bottom when free spooled, providing an action that no other lure can duplicate.

FLOAT AND CLACKER RIGS

The float rig is popular along the mid-Atlantic and Northeast coasts to keep bottom-fishing baits away from pesky crabs. The float looks like a regular ordinary lead-head bucktail until you pick it up and realize it's made of balsa wood or Styrofoam. The fanciest of them boast nice-looking paint jobs and have some bucktail hair tied around the hook shank, but a plain Jane all-white version will work just as well.

Weakfish and sea trout love sea worms presented on float rigs. The rig is somewhat similar to a three-way rig, but the float keeps the bait suspended 2 to 3 feet off the bottom to keep blue claw crabs from eating it. The soft bait can be a whole worm, in which case tiderunner weakfish or striped bass may also show some interest, or for smaller weaks and trout, 3- to 4-inch pieces of worm can be draped to the hook. Croaker, snappers, ladyfish, pompano and flounder will jump on this rig too, especially when a shrimp or curly-tail soft bait is used in place of the worm.

Use a slender freshwater-style rubber worm or a natural-looking sandworm, such as Berkley Gulp! 2- and 4-inch sandworms. Soft-plastic squid, peeler crabs and sand fleas (sand crabs) are other excellent candidates to bait a float rig.

The clacker rig is an old-time favorite that has recently begun to enjoy renewed popularity. The float rides on a short length of wire so it slides freely back and forth. Metal beads are placed at each end of the wire so when the float is jerked or popped, it crashes into a bead and makes a clacking sound. The soft bait, such as a shrimp, crab, jerkbait, worm or curly tail trails behind the float on an 18- to 30-inch leader.

SPINNER TROLLING RIG

If you remember Elvis, you also remember that the original rubber worm sold in tackle shops sported two to three hooks rigged in tandem along the body of the worm, and the rig usually had a spinner blade flashing at the front. It's a rare event to see a worm rigged this way today, yet coastal fishermen are trying new versions of this venerable rig and brag of some great catches of striped bass and snook, sometimes weakfish with a worm trolling rig.

Trolling rigs can be made with either one hook or two, and a spinner blade up front. Even in the darkness of night, the spinner blade reflects a muted flash from the moonlight or nearby shore lights that helps striped bass home in on the bait. The blade also transmits vibration and a clinking sound into the surrounding water which adds to the appeal of the lure; powerful scent, lifelike visual attraction, flash and sound vibration—it's an irresistible bait!

A double-hook soft-plastic worm rig with a spinner blade up front is a traditional favorite that catches spring and summer school stripers—weakfish, too.

There are two popular ways to rig a trolling bait with a single hook. One is based on the traditional Texas rig with a Z-hook, including the optional nose weight if you need to get a few feet below the surface; and the other uses a straight-shank Sproat-style J-hook rigged at the nose of the worm. Some sharpies will rig two worms on the same Sproat hook, one worm slipped onto the shank of the hook, the second worm hooked through the nose so it is positioned on the bend of the hook. The two worms flutter and undulate, pushed and tugged by the natural action of the sea water as it flows over the bodies of the worms. Mmm, mmm, good!

A double-hook rig is easily made by snelling the tail hook onto a 24-inch length of 20- or 30-pound mono, then using a separate piece of mono to snell the second hook into place several inches in front of the tail hook. Because it is snelled with a separate piece of mono, the front hook can be slid along the leader to adjust the hook position of any length worm. Owner and SPRO offer these rigs pre-made in several hook sizes and a variety of leader strengths. When rigging a double-hook trolling rig, be sure the hooks are in perfect alignment, otherwise you'll have an enormous line-twist problem. To further avoid line twist, a small Krok or SPRO barrel swivel can be added at the forward end of the leader.

There are several types of spinner blades that work well, and the rigging hardware is available at most tackle shops. The big, rounded shape of the Colorado spinner is a good choice, but the all-time favorite is the Cape Cod spinner, a double willow-leaf style, rigged on a short stainless steel wire mount. A single willow-leaf spinner will also work.

What makes the trolling rig so deadly is the expanded selection of sea worm-type baits now available from several manufacturers. In particular, Berkley's 8-inch PowerBait Sandworm and the 6- and 8-inch Gulp! Sandworm are such realistic looking baits that you'd swear they were raked from the worm beds of Maine. Trolled slowly at night along a sedge bank or a rocky cove, this bait is a killer for school to medium-size stripers. Not only does the bait have PowerBait and Gulp!'s exceptional scent, they are molded to perfectly duplicate a real sandworm.

4

LEADHEADS, BUCKTAILS, AND SWIMBAITS

The use of bucktails as fishing lures goes back to ancient times as evidenced by the bucktail-type lures found preserved in ancient Egyptian tombs. Thousands of years later, the bucktail is still doing yeoman duty all along the coast catching plenty of fish and making the traditional bucktail the top contender as one of the great fishing lures of all time.

A leadhead draped with a plastic worm is a traditional soft-bait presentation for many inshore gamefish, including striped bass, snook, and weakfish like this big tiderunner.

Old-timers called them doodlebugs, and they fished "bugs" in the surf, from jetties, at inlets, in back bays and rivers, along the inshore waters and over deep wrecks. If any lure could claim to be a universal fish catcher, doodlebug bucktails were it. Of course, they still catch fish today, and if you add a soft-plastic tail you have a lure that is absolutely hard to beat. The natural pulsating action of the bucktail hair and the soft action and profile of the plastic tail make a winning combination—no wonder saltwater fish of all sizes eat them!

Sometimes simple is better and many anglers no longer bother with the bucktail dressing, they just fish a plain, unadorned lead jig head with a soft-plastic tail pushed over the hook. While the color variations of a painted head can be important to some anglers, many others prefer to fish unpainted leadheads, relying on the soft tail to add all the color that is needed to attract a strike.

The latest evolution of the ancient bucktail is today's modern swimbait with a plastic body molded around the leadhead. Bucktail or plain, painted or not, this family of lures enjoys a reputation for catching fish that includes spike sea trout and pompano of only a pound or two to immense amberjack and yellowfin tuna. A properly presented bucktail, leadhead or swimbait is tough for a hungry game fish to pass up. The key is in presenting the lure to the fish so they want to attack it.

Leadheads, bucktails and swimbaits can be trolled, but they are the most fun to fish when the angler breathes life into them by casting to the edge of a marsh sedge, a school of feeding fish or when jigging over a wreck or drop-off into deeper water. Manipulating the rod tip, making the lure dance and dart is an exciting way to fish— it's an art form when executed by a skilled guide or local pro with years of experience fooling game fish with leadhead lures.

They catch fish all year long; there really is no season when they can't catch fish. In the coolest of winter water temperatures, a slow crawling retrieve will still fool gamefish, and if the retrieve speed is adjusted for changing water temperatures, this family of lures works just as well in spring, summer and fall conditions.

IT'S ALL IN YOUR HEAD

Bucktails, leadheads and swimbaits are sold with a wide variety of head shapes and profiles to imitate the silhouette of the most common natural baits, or to imitate their specific swimming action. Fishermen from one part of the East Coast tend to favor one or two styles of head shapes over others, while their counterparts along a different part of the coast may favor something much different; but it's interesting to note that they all work wherever you try them. The fat profile of a peanut bunker found along the Northeast and mid-Atlantic looks much the same as Florida's scaled sardine and thread herring.

Among the most popular head shapes are the time-tested lima bean popularized by the long-gone Upperman Company, the round musket ball, open-mouth Smilin' Bill, torpedo and the bullet shape. Each style has its fans depending on which bay, sound or coastal area is being fished, and there is a wide selection of variations on each of these designs. As an example, the Owner catalog lists 11 different leadhead shapes; the Do-It Molds catalog lists over 40! Most tackle shops carry a wide assortment of many different head shapes, and manufacturers of soft baits all have their own versions of leadhead shapes to get the best action.

The shape of the leadhead influences the action of the lure and how fast it sinks. Some heads work best with an aggressive rod action, others with something more subtle.

It is amazing how one head shape can sometimes be so much better catching fish than another, and at other times it seems to matter very little which head shape is used. One of my favorite haunts for school stripers was locked into a pattern that seemed unshakeable for several days; white and chartreuse SPRO bucktails with a white twister tail were the hot item and nothing else caught with any consistency or predictability, yet on one day the SPRO bugs became powerless to fool a fish. I tried several alternatives and finally began catching on a D.O.A. leadhead with a silver-fleck shad tail. What happened? The small bay anchovies were displaced with pods of peanut bunker and the bass stopped striking on slim-profile bucktails and switched to a lure with a fatter, peanut bunker profile. The silver-fleck tail more closely resembled the natural color of the peanuts under the bridge lights and the pulsating tail had all the action needed to attract strike after strike. The message; be ready to experiment because just when you think you've figured the fish out, they throw you a curve ball.

While head shape can be important because of the profile it presents to a game fish, probably more important is the balance of the leadhead in relation to the attachment eye because this controls the retrieve action of the lure. Its position will add to, or take away from, the lure's action as it is cast and retrieved, trolled or jigged.

Some leadheads and swimbaits place the hook eye near the nose of the lure; others place it about one-third back from the nose, or halfway back. Some lures even have two hook-eye positions so the same lure can be fished in two different retrieve styles. There is no single "ideal" attachment position; each variation produces a different action that can be better in one fishing situation than another.

With the hook eye at the nose, the plastic tail of the bucktail, leadhead or swimbait will hang at a downward angle below the nose when the lure is at rest. When cast out and away from the angler, and then retrieved with short twitches of the rod tip, the swimbait will dart and hop nicely. The natural drag of the water as the lure is pulled toward the angler will keep the tail riding nearly parallel to the bottom. The lure will dance with a short hopping action that looks extremely life like.

When jigged vertically in deep water, lures with the hook eye positioned far forward, work with an extreme up-and-down action of the tail, which may not be as realistic as a more natural hopping action. In deep water, many fishermen look for baits with the hook placed farther back on the lure head. The lure then tends to ride parallel to the bottom with a less severe hopping action. Bridge, dock and pier fishermen especially like this action, but keep

This striped bass hit a large soft bait fished by Gary Caputi of the Recreational Fishing Alliance on a heavy leadhead with the attachment eye positioned far forward for enhanced vertical jigging action.

in mind that the fish may at times prefer the more wild action. It pays to have both types of heads in your tackle bag.

Leadheads that concentrate their weight far forward can be retrieved with a hop-and-lift jigging action such as the musket ball style. Draped with a plastic worm tail, this leadhead has enjoyed a reputation that spans nearly 40 years of catching weakfish over the shallow shoals of Delaware Bay and along the inshore coastal waters for croaker, summer flounder and striped bass. The D.O.A. TerrorEyze with its bug-eye lead weight has similar action and is hopped with vertical lifts of the rod tip to catch pompano, jacks, snook, reds and sea trout. It is a favorite for fishing bridges and around dock pilings where snook lie in wait for a quick snack, and it does a great job on bridge stripers up north. Both lures use their inherent weight-forward balance to create their famous action that drives gamefish nuts.

The rhythm or pulse rate of the jigging action is another essential component of the retrieve. Sand eels dart and zip from side to side so a bullet-shaped jig retrieved in a series of short sweeps will imitate this silvery baitfish better than a slow, hopping action. Spearing, shrimp and sand fleas move in shorter darts and often appear to glide, then hop, as they move with tide and current. A lima-bean or musket-ball bucktail retrieved in shorter hops will get more interest than a long sweeping retrieve. The variety of retrieves is nearly endless and it pays to experiment with different actions on every fishing trip.

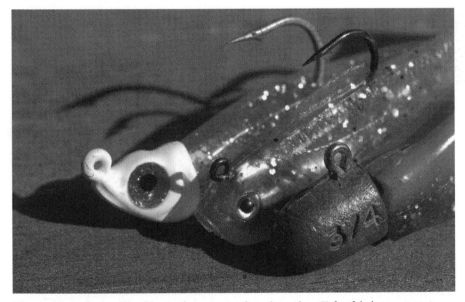

The position of a leadhead's attachment eye alters its action. Take this into account when selecting heads for vertical jigging, shallow water and bridge fishing.

Subtle differences in the retrieve rhythm can influence fishing success. Two anglers standing side by side, fishing identical lures and tackle rigging, may not catch fish at the same pace if their rhythm is not the same. I saw this on hundreds of occasions while I was actively charter fishing and I'm certain of its validity.

Speed of retrieve is important too. Spring-run weakfish, sea trout and striped bass are still feeling the effects of cold water and will not feed as aggressively as they will in the warmer summer months. A fast retrieve will be ignored no matter how hungry they may be.

Linda Barrett worked a pink jerkbait and leadhead with a moderate retrieve speed. The fish were lying up close to the beach in the wash chasing sand eels.

To slow the retrieve down, boat-fishing anglers cast leadheads and bucktails into the direction of the drift. The drifting boat moving towards the retrieved bucktail tends to slow the lure down.

Bluefish or crevalle jacks chasing a school of bait will laugh at a slow moving lure. Give them too much time to examine the lure and they'll probably be able to tell where you bought it and how much you paid for it! A fast moving lead jig will get more results.

The level of retrieve, or the depth of the lure in the water column, is also critical. Surface feeding gamefish are exciting to cast to, yet a lure retrieved near the surface may get few strikes. Allowing the lure to sink at least a few feet will get more strikes. Weakfish, white perch, striped bass, sea trout and summer flounder need a lure retrieved near or on the bottom. The tail-hanging bucktails can be hopped or bounced along the bottom with deadly results. Work the rod tip in short vertical lifts to get the bucktail dancing. On the down stroke of the rod, the lure should hit the bottom and bounce up on the next rod lift.

The weight of the leadhead or bucktail can be critical. You only need enough weight to hit the bottom. Too much weight may ruin the action of the lure. Not enough weight will leave the lure at the mercy of tide or current and never allow it to get to the fish. Surface or near surface retrieves call for enough weight for casting convenience. Leadheads bounced on a channel edge or deep shoal need enough weight to cut through the current to get to the bottom. Naturally the weight of the leadhead should match the tackle being used. A 3-ounce bucktail is hardly the lure for a one-handed casting rod meant for ¾-ounce lures.

GETTING IN SHAPE

Equally important as the shape of the leadhead, is the shape of the soft-plastic tails—and there are plenty from which to choose. Slender jerkbaits, round-bodied paddle tails, plump shads, vibrating curly tails, worms and shrimp can all be added to a bucktail or leadhead, and not to be outdone, swimbaits are readily available with these same tail styles.

The shape of the plastic tail offers variations in lure action, from subtle wiggles such as with a paddle tail or curly tail to the more aggressive wild darts of a jerkbait. The most popular tail shape is the standard swim shad tail, also called a paddle tail. This shape offers

This long, eel-like worm fished on a leadhead was just the ticket for a weakfish that thought it had an easy meal.

plenty of wiggling motion that can excite gamefish to strike. Another popular tail shape is the slender, jointed tail that acts like a snapping shrimp. A slender split-tail shape resembles a sand eel, spearing or bay anchovy, while fat little dudes imitate a pinfish or porgy. The time-tested twister or curly tail is also a top performer.

Any fisherman with saltwater experience will vouch for the importance of color, and can probably recite a dozen stories to prove when one color bucktail worked a lot better than another color. One of my experiences occurred on a trip to Long Island's Great South Bay for weakfish. I was using a white bug with a pink Mister Twister tail and caught fish after fish while my partner failed to get a hook up. He tried several colors, but didn't have a pink tail in his tackle box. I finally relented and gave him a pink Twister—his rod was soon bent to a nice weakfish, proof positive that color, at least on that day, was the key ingredient to success. Color may play a big part in the success of any fishing day so I always have a selection of proven colors in my tackle bag.

Thankfully, the saltwater soft-plastic fisherman can choose from a nearly limitless array of colors to imitate virtually any natural baitfish color scheme from mackerel to menhaden, bright attractor colors like pink and chartreuse, and subtle colors like purple and motor oil green. At the right time, they all have their moment of glory.

RIGGING 'EM RIGHT

Sliding a plastic tail onto a leadhead is both simple and critical. Do it hastily and the tail will be incorrectly aligned or bent so the lure rides on its side, or slide the tail too high on the hook and it will look like an imposter to the fish. If it looks "funny," you'll get few, if any, strikes. This is especially true with thin jerkbaits like the Fin-S Fish and Bass Assassin and some thin profile shad tails, but it is less critical with thicker, more rounded body shad tails, curly tails, Slug-Go baits, squids and jumbo worms.

To assure proper position of the plastic along the leadhead's hook shank, lay the tail alongside the leadhead to get a good idea of exactly how the tail will fit. As a quick reference, you can use the hook point to poke a small hole in the back of the tail as a visual aid to help determine where to push the hook point out of the bait. Some soft tails have the manufacturer's name molded into the back of the plastic body and these letters serve as a handy reference.

When pushing the plastic tail onto the hook, be sure the hook point is being inserted into the very center of the tail, not off to one side which would then cause the bait to retrieve awkwardly. I find it's better to start with a short push with the bait held firmly between my thumb and forefinger.

Use your forefinger to help slide the soft bait around the bend of the leadhead's hook. Be sure to keep the hook point and hook shank centered exactly in the bait.

Once the tail is slid far enough onto the hook point and it's time to begin bending the bait, change the position of your fingers so the bait is held between the thumb and the index finger, and the forefinger is now in a position so your three fingers form a triangle. The forefinger now helps to bend the bait around the hook bend while

Like the Boy Scouts, it pays to be prepared. Have a good selection of jigheads in several sizes and weights, backed up with a variety of tails in different shapes, sizes and colors.

the thumb and index finger continues to push the bait further along the hook.

Before completely seating the tail onto the hook shank, some anglers like to add a drop of CA glue for an extra dose of holding power. Short-striking fish can pull the tail rearward on the hook shank causing it to ride at an angle—not good. Usually the tail can be slid back into position after a short strike and can be fished again, but two or more short strikes will wear out the inside of the tail and it will no longer hold firmly on the hook—that's the time to replace the tail.

Draping a plastic tail on a leadhead or bucktail is probably the most common and popular way to fish soft baits in saltwater. From Texas to Maine, virtually every fisherman will have the jig heads and the plastic tails that are the most popular to local gamefish. The many colors, shapes, sizes and silhouettes make them ideal for shallow flats, back bay, near shore and offshore—it's the universal way to fish soft plastic lures.

HOW TO FISH 'EM

Let's spend a bit more time discussing how to get the most fish-catching action from leadheads, bucktails and swimbaits. In many respects these are "do-nothing" lures. Were it not for the vibrating tails on some of them, they literally have no action whatsoever and rely to a great extent on the angler's ability to jig the lure to breathe life into it. The manipulation of the lure is accomplished by the combination of many variables. A gentle flick of the wrist or the long sweep of the arm imparts action to the lure through the motion of the fishing rod. A quick or slow retrieve is accomplished by the choice of a high-speed reel or by fast, energetic cranking of the reel handle. The angle of the lure to the bottom structure, whether straight up and down, at 45 degrees or if cast far out and retrieved in shallow water all have a bearing on how effective the lure will be.

Al Reinfelder, in his excellent book, *Bait Tail Fishing*, developed the concept of the jigging equation, and nearly 40 years later his thoughts still ring true. According to Al, the jigging equation is composed of four parts; speed, jigging frequency, distance and force. By altering any one or more of these important aspects, the jigging action can be infinitely varied to make the lure dance in a manner that will excite gamefish and trigger a strike.

JIGGING EQUATION = SPEED + FREQUENCY
+ DISTANCE + FORCE

Okay, his concept was already subconsciously in use by thousands of fishermen along the coast for decades, but Al was the first to put the theory into writing so it could be studied and discussed by veteran and experienced anglers, and taught to new anglers.

Retrieving the lure is often called "working" the lure and it's the working of the lure that gets the fish's attention and the strike. It is the very essence of fishing a leadhead, bucktail or swimbait. Making the lure come alive to fool a big snook, striped bass, trout or weakfish is challenging and rewarding, but not really all that difficult if you develop your jigging equation and fishing strategy carefully. It's what makes fishing leadheads and soft plastics so much fun.

SPEED is controlled by the slow or aggressive cranking of the reel handle, and also in part by the reel's gear ratio. In situations where a slow retrieve is needed, a high-speed reel may actually be an impediment to successful fishing. A reel with a moderate gear ratio is usually more versatile than a reel with a ripping-fast high-speed ratio, but this is partly due to personal preference. Some anglers have an easier time coordinating their hand movement when speeding up a reel by cranking faster, instead of slowing down their hand movement to crank slower.

Current and speed of drift also are a factor when determining jigging speed. A lure traveling with the current, or with the drift, is actually moving slower because the boat is moving toward the lure while the angler is cranking the handle. Casting a lure into the back side of the drift will speed it up slightly because the current is trying to pull the lure away from the angler. If your typical cranking retrieve is 3 knots, and the drift speed is 1 knot; casting into the drift will move the lure towards the angler at 2 knots (3-knot reel speed, minus 1-knot drift speed), but casting to the back of the drift will move the lure at 4 knots (3-knot reel speed, plus 1-knot drift speed).

The type and pound test of line you use will also influence the jigging equation. Small diameter monofilament and super braids tend to cut through the water with much less water resistance than a large diameter mono line. A large diameter will cause the lure to ride higher, and will inhibit its sink rate.

FREQUENCY describes the number of times you move the rod tip to make the lure dart. The most basic jigging frequency, one which many fishermen use without really being conscious of it is the "jig-one thousand, jig-two thousand" cadence. This is basically, a jig of the rod tip approximately every second, and from this standard count many variations can be created, including a steady jigging motion or an erratic motion.

DISTANCE describes the length of the lure's travel during the jigging motion. A short flick of the wrist moves the leadhead along a

A slow-speed, regular jigging action with short, gentle lifts of the rod tip was the ideal jigging equation to catch this shallow-water summer flounder.

shorter distance than does a long sweep of the rod tip. The distance of the lure movement can be varied by the angler and it can be steady or erratic, such as a long rod sweep followed by two short motions. The trick is to make the lure look like a fleeing, injured or unknowing target for a gamefish.

FORCE refers to the power you exert during the jigging motion. The motion can be a gentle flick of the wrist for a subtle hopping action, or an aggressive, forceful pull that darts the jig with a lot of power.

All four factors influence the motion of the lure, and when combined perfectly, they come together in such a way that fish have a tough time refusing to strike. Remember that each of the factors can be varied independent of the others. As examples; you can speed up the retrieve without changing the rhythm of the jigging frequency, distance or force; or change the jigging frequency without altering the overall retrieve speed, distance or force.

The importance of finding the best jigging motion for any given fishing day is vital to your success. The standard jig-one thousand, jig-two thousand rhythm is always a good place to start, and if it works (which it usually does) don't experiment. The time to try new retrieves is when the fish aren't biting! The success of one angler over another is often due to subtle variations. One of my favorite

Captain Ed Zyak of Jensen Beach was dialed in with a moderate-speed retrieve and a steady jigging rhythm with short hops to score this decent-size Indian River trout.

bridge-fishing locations seems to produce school stripers when I use a steady retrieve with occasional short, gentle jigs of the leadhead. I fish this location so frequently that the retrieve and the jigging equation for it is second nature and I'm not really conscious of the way the lure is moving. If I ask a buddy to fish this spot, he may not catch at the same pace as I do until he gets that special rhythm down pat.

This frequently happens to all fishermen, as shown by a trip I recall with Captain Ed Zyak, one of Stuart, Florida's premier guides, where his hook-up ratio on speckled trout was so much better than mine because of the little nuances he dialed into his retrieve. After eagle-eyeing his technique, my catch frequency quickly got much better, and proved once again that if you're not catching, and the other guy is, carefully check out his technique. If all other things are equal—lure size, color and weight—chances are the retrieve equation is the key.

Do-Nothing Jigging

Some baitfish move through the water, or simply maintain a steady position in the current, with very little visible movement or tail action. For this reason, a steady, do-nothing jigging retrieve often works very well when fishing leadheads, bucktails and swimbaits. This technique is especially good with those lures with paddle or curly tails that develop their own action independently of any jigging or darting motion of the lure. A straight-in, do-nothing retrieve can be an excellent basic retrieve choice.

I use this technique when fishing bridges, in inlets, along shoals and deep holes and when fish are holding in rips; letting the lure swing with the current, and maintaining its position just ahead of a bridge piling or abutment before cranking the reel to retrieve the lure for the next cast. Many times, striped bass and snook will smack a lure that just sits there in the current. Unknown to the angler in the boat or on the shore, the lure is probably undulating and moving slightly in the current, just like a live natural baitfish and that's why the strike occurs.

The do-nothing retrieve is also effective when fishing very shallow water when even the slightest pause might allow the leadhead to plunge a few inches into grassy weeds, a mussel bed or a rocky bottom where it can snag or foul. Keeping the rod tip high will help keep the lure tangle- and snag-free.

Steady, Regular Jigging

When you hear a catchy tune, you want to tap your foot to the beat; when you cast a leadhead it's also just as natural to add a little jigging action to the retrieve. It must be ingrained in every fisherman's subconscious that a leadhead must be jigged; at least, just a little bit. The steady, regular jigging rhythm is a good one and is probably the most frequently used retrieve action.

Regular jigging means that you follow a fixed pattern with equal pauses in between the jigging action. Like the catchy tune, the "beat" is regular or evenly spaced, and so is the jigging action of the leadhead when the steady, regular retrieve is used. The jigging can be fast or slow, gentle or hard, but it is steady and evenly spaced throughout the entire retrieve from the time the lure splashes down on the water until it's at the rod tip ready for the next cast.

Let's consider again the jig-one thousand, jig-two thousand retrieve, since this is the most often used jigging rhythm. Many gamefish will aggressively strike at this retrieve; snook, stripers, weakfish, flounder, bonito, cobia—virtually every important game fish will smack a soft-plastic lure retrieved with a steady, regular jigging motion. Why do they do this? A close look at undisturbed schools of bait will show that they travel in much the same manner with a steady movement and occasional darts and short speed ups. The steady, regular retrieve imitates this natural of the baitfish, therefore, it works.

Erratic Jigging

With this retrieve formula, the angler changes any or all of the jigging equation factors; speed, jigging frequency, distance and force. The cranking speed can be varied, and the rod is manipulated so the lure is always changing its darting action. A typical erratic retrieve might start off with a long rod sweep, followed by a steady retrieve, then two short hops, and then a long rod sweep again. The jigging action alternates between gentle pulses of the rod tip to long, hard sweeps of the rod tip, or any other combination that the angler believes will work.

Rich Barrett (right) worked a chartreuse C.A.L. shad tail at a fast speed and with aggressive jigging to catch the attention of this crevalle jack.

The erratic retrieve represents a disturbed baitfish; a bait that is wounded or injured, stunned, escaping or unpredictable. The tiny brain of a baitfish has no concept of fear, but its survival instincts are highly tuned and it will react in a wild, disoriented manner when trying to flee for its life. A lethargic game fish may take advantage of this opportunity to take a swipe at a baitfish that appears to be in trouble.

While most experienced fishermen rely on and believe that the power of the steady, regular jigging motion is superior, the erratic retrieve can be useful at times and is a good technique to keep in your bag of tricks when other retrieves fail.

Hopping Jigging
This is really a variation of the steady, regular jigging action, but with the rod tip held at 45 degrees to the water. When the soft-plastic bait is jigged by flicking the wrist and moving the rod tip upward, the lure darts upward and then plunges down at the pause before the next movement of the rod tip draw the lure upwards again.

This hopping-retrieve technique works especially well in relatively shallow water for stripers, snook, jacks, pompano, redfish and trout. In Pamlico Sound, North Carolina or Long Island's Great South Bay, it's a go-to method that fools plenty of fish. Leadheads with the eye positioned far forward are good choices for this style of retrieve. With the balance point and the weight concentrated forward, these leadheads develop a terrific hopping action and are favorite choices all along the coast.

Vertical Jigging

A more dramatic version of the hopping jigging described above, vertical jigging is best when the lure is jigged along the bottom and the lure's position is maintained directly below the boat and with minimal scope in the line. Because it is essential for the lure to be on the bottom, not rising several feet above it, the leadhead must have enough weight to stay on the bottom. After each rod lift, if you can't feel the lure bouncing the bottom when the rod tip is lowered, you need a heavier leadhead.

When vertical jigging the lure is not cast, it's simply free-spooled to the bottom. You'll feel a "thump" transmitted through the line to the rod blank as the lure hits bottom. Start the vertical jigging with the rod tip pointed low at the water then lift the rod tip upward about 2 to 3 feet if you're in deep water, or just a foot or two in shallow water. The rod tip will sweep the lure off the bottom, much like a baitfish being chased by a predator, and it will catch the attention of nearby gamefish.

Doubleheader! Ben Secrest and Shimano's Ted Sakai were deep jigging off Key West when a pair of donkey-size AJs grabbed their jigs. Soft plastics draped on heavy heads go deep and plumb the depths.

This technique works well for bottom feeders like summer flounder, sea bass and grouper over a reef or wreck, stripers on a shoal or sand bar, snook in an inlet or trout and weakfish along a channel edge. It also works for dolphin stationed around a fish trap marker or weed line, and for big-bad tuna that will strike at a vertical jigged soft plastic when dropped down deep in a chum slick.

Vertical jigging is deadly on summer flounder and a lot of fun. Use it in water only 3 feet deep or 30 feet deep, and each time the jolting strikes will get you grinning. It's a lot more fun than just dragging a squid strip along the bottom waiting for a strike—duh!

So, here's the big question, "Which retrieve is best?" The answer is easy; "They all are!" But, the ultimate decision is always made by the fish, and for reasons unknown to fishermen, gamefish will sometimes prefer a slight variation of the standard retrieve that you use all the time. That's why it is so critical on those days when you experience a slow bite to keep your mind open to trying subtle or dramatically new retrieve equations. Each retrieve variation will have its day in the sun, its moment of glory when it works better than any other technique or jigging rhythm and the fish seem to strike on every cast.

I always start out with my standard steady regular jigging because it works most of the time, but if the bites aren't coming, it's time to experiment.

5

SENSATIONAL SHRIMP, COOL CRABS

Man, there's nothing quite like having a secret weapon to fool fish; a lure so good that even on a dog day it will turn your best fishing buddy green with envy as you pick away at snook and trout, or striped bass and weakfish. Good days and slow days, for many shallow-water anglers and guides, artificial shrimp are just such a secret weapon.

Fake shrimp enjoy a tremendous and growing popularity with anglers in Florida and along the Gulf coast, but to be consistently successful, you must learn techniques that breathe life into these soft-plastic creations; and that makes all the fish-catching difference in the world. Mid-Atlantic and Northeast fishermen don't usually bother to fish with artificial shrimp because bait shops don't even handle live shrimp, especially the further north along the coast you travel. For many up-coast anglers the questions is, "If I can't buy the real deal in a bait shop, why would I fish an imitation?"

Well, there are many good reasons to fish an artificial shrimp, whether you fish in Florida or Connecticut, but to get the most from any lure you have to have confidence that it will work. Anglers who have taken the time to learn the nuances and the magic of fishing with artificial shrimp can make them work as good, sometimes better, than a live one. At times the number of fish they catch can be astonishing. Wading near a causeway bridge in Stuart, Florida along-side Captain Marcia Foosaner, one of the area's top guides, the two of us caught and released several dozen snook and trout in about an hour's time. No live bait was used, only a silver-speckled, ¼-ounce artificial D.O.A. shrimp. We kept a few spares in reserve in our shirt pockets just in case we got ambushed and chewed up by a toothy critter, but the entire catch was made on artificials.

I was lucky to get some tutoring from Captain Mark Nichols, and the lessons learned from the "master" have been put to good use in the Indian River and Hobe Sound for snook, trout, jacks, ladies and redfish; and in Barnegat Bay for a mixed bag of school striped bass, weakfish and fluke. As an example, one late afternoon drift fishing near the big bay's Oyster Creek power plant outlet, I fished a D.O.A. chartreuse, ¼-ounce shrimp, casting it along the edge of a marsh drop-off a few yards to the north of the creek's mouth. The striped bass were lying along the shallow edge of the drop-off and I walloped five stripers in about 30 minutes. These were nice plump spring bass including a 30-inch keeper.

It's not just a southern thing—artificial shrimp are deadly on school stripers from Virginia to Maine, and they catch weakfish and fluke, too.

I tossed a sample shrimp to another angler who was crowding my drift after the third fish, and got one of those "are you kidding?" looks as he caught the fake shrimp I had pitched over to him. He put the shrimp on the console of his boat and continued casting his swimming plug. I wonder if he ever tried the shrimp. He should have because school stripers and spring-run weakfish have a hard time passing up a juicy shrimp—even if it is fake!

Mark was not surprised when I told him the story. "I've fished D.O.A. shrimp in the Northeast and Virginia, and they catch plenty of stripers, and weakfish, too. People just don't think of shrimp as a good bait up north, so they don't try them." If you aren't yet a believer, make this the season to try them.

EXACT DUPLICATES

There are several species of shrimp found along the coast, and they are a primary food source for most gamefish. The best artificial shrimp are incredibly accurate imitations of the real thing. In the Gulf and along the Florida and Atlantic coasts, the common shrimp is the most prevalent. It's the same shrimp served peel-n-eat style at a beach café or Parmesan-style at an Italian restaurant. The much smaller grass shrimp is found by the millions along dock pilings, in back-bay grass beds and tidal marshes. There's also a nasty dude called the mantis shrimp that will draw blood if it nips your finger. Add in the many other "shrimpy looking" crustaceans to the buffet menu, and it's easy to see that shrimp-like food is readily available for snook and stripers from Massachusetts to the Florida Keys and Texas.

With all these shrimp and shrimp look-alikes, the idea of casting an artificial shrimp lure makes good sense. Fortunately, there is a wide variety of imposter shrimp manufactured in several sizes, a wide selection of colors, and which can be purchased pre-rigged as a natural-looking shrimp and unrigged to be draped to a leadhead or Z-hook.

NATURAL RIGGING

A natural-rigged shrimp is a very deadly lure. Each is factory-rigged so the bait sinks slowly much like a natural live shrimp. The weight is positioned in the belly of the bait so it rides hook up. There's no action to the lure until the angler twitches the rod tip and makes the lure jump, dart, swim or hop.

Unlike a shrimp rigged on a leadhead, natural-rigged shrimp work best with a slow, casual stop-and-go retrieve. The goal is to make the shrimp look alive. Shrimp usually move slowly with a steady, lazy motion, and only dart quickly when frightened or attacked. You'll get more hook-ups if after casting the shrimp, you let it settle, then slowly lift the rod tip to gently twitch the shrimp. Reel in any slack, let the lure settle again, and continue the twitch, reel and pause retrieve. This is the same technique Captain Rick Grassett uses for trout, reds and snook around Sarasota, and he told me, "A slow, gentle retrieve takes patience, but it can be amazingly effective and very hard for any respectable gamefish to pass up."

Other fishermen prefer to retrieve the shrimp with erratic twitches of the rod tip and at a much faster pace. While not as successful as the lazy approach, it does work from time to time and can be an "ace in the hole" on those days when the slow retrieve is ignored.

A special, unique retrieve developed by Captain Mark Benson to fish the very shallow waters of Florida's Mosquito Lagoon keeps the

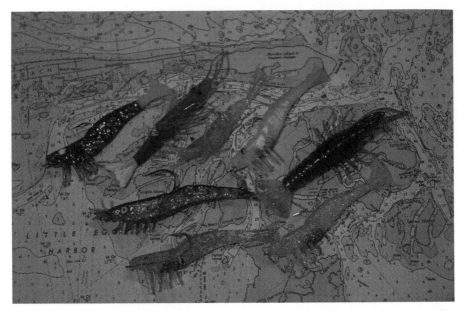

Artificial shrimp are hot lures along most of the Gulf and southern coasts for trout, reds and snook, and also work well in the mid-Atlantic areas for striped bass and weakfish.

lure on the surface and throws a wake that catches the attention of snook, sea trout and redfish. He nicknamed the technique "minesweeping" and it is a very effective method to fool northern gamefish too. After watching Mark I've tried the technique in Barnegat Bay and the Manasquan River and scored on striped bass holding near shallow sand bars and mussel beds at the last hour of the outgoing or the start of the incoming when the current is not yet flowing real hard.

To get the most action when minesweeping, begin the retrieve by cranking the reel handle soon as the shrimp hits the water at the end of the cast. Crank only fast enough to keep the lure on the surface, which is not very fast, and complete the retrieve with no rod action at all. This retrieve works at its best when the surface water is very calm, and especially at dawn and dusk when the water is flat-calm and the fish can home in on the wake.

When fishing near bridges, the shrimp can be cast directly at a piling and allowed to sink, then twitched back with a slow retrieve; or cast at 90 degrees from the boat or wading position and allowed to swing with the current, again twitching the lure with the rod tip. This technique works best when the current is not at full speed, so I use it at the change of the tide; the first hour and a half of the beginning of either the incoming or outgoing is usually good, and so is the last half hour of the incoming and outgoing.

Use the swing technique when casting to striped bass holding along a sandy point, or at an opening in a sand bar. The shrimp looks like it was washed over the bar and usually gets the fish's attention. Cast at 90 degrees to the current direction and let the shrimp float and drift with the current until the line begins to tighten and as the line straightens. This is the sweet spot that often gets the strikes.

Skipping a shrimp under a dock is another unique technique that once learned is extremely effective. It can be used in daylight, especially in areas with overhanging mangroves, but it's really a

Spencer Hobby learned his shrimp-skipping skills from his dad, Captain Paul Hobby. He caught this hefty snook by casting an artificial shrimp into a mangrove edge. D.O.A. Lures photo.

hot technique at night when throwing an artificial shrimp under a lighted dock. You can often see snook milling around the pilings, but these are usually the smaller fish, the bigger fish will be stationed well under the dock and protected.

The skip cast is a modified version of a side-arm cast and it's a great technique to avoid snagging and hanging the lure up on the dock, where a standard overhead cast is nearly useless. The side-arm cast keeps the lure's trajectory low to the water so the shrimp can be rocketed to land far under the dock. Captain Paul Hobby's son, Spencer, skillfully demonstrated the technique early one morning at oh-dark-thirty when we fished around several snook infested docks along Sewall's Point on the St. Lucie River before first light. Spencer used a circular flip of the rod tip to underhand the sidearm cast and make the shrimp hit the water a few feet from the edge of the dock. The momentum of the cast kept the shrimp traveling for one, two or three more skips until it settled far beneath the dock. Hungry snook, hearing and seeing this natural-looking disturbance, eagerly ate the baits and Spence was hooked-up several times with decent-size snook that morning well before we took a break at dawn to relax for a few moments before looking for some bridge fishing action.

Skipping a shrimp under a dock, although a southern technique, works just fine up north. School striped bass will hold around docks in New England, Long Island, New Jersey and the Outer Banks and can be caught with this same method. Several productive docks in my home waters on the Manasquan River have given up striped bass that could not resist a skipped shrimp.

Some shrimp are manufactured with a unique action of their own. The Storm WildEye Rattle Shrimp is rigged to look like a natural, but has an unusual jointed body configuration. A rattle and weight are rigged in such a way that the tail snaps and flips when the rod tip is manipulated. The action is enticing and very lifelike. Retrieved with short rod twitches, this shrimp will take fluke, weakies and bass in shallow water, and southern snook, reds, trout and jacks.

Another technique that works well just about anywhere along the coast is the clacker rig, or popper rig. The natural-rigged shrimp is tied about 3 feet behind a special clacker or sound-making float that slides an inch or two along a through wire, which is tied to the end of the main fishing line. The shrimp suspends realistically below the float. To catch the attention of a nearby snook or striped bass, jerk the rod tip to make the float splash and clack. Skeptics are usu-

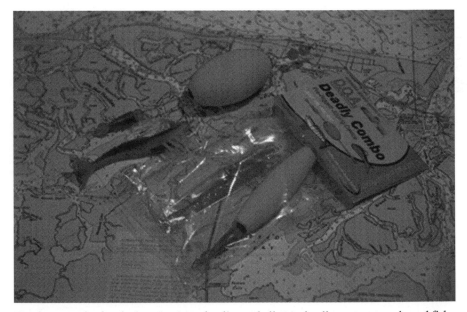

North or south, the clacker rig rings the dinner bell. It's deadly on trout and weakfish, and it catches the attention of many other gamefish, too.

ally surprised at how well the rig catches fish, especially trout and weakfish, when they give it a serious try. It has saved the night for me on several occasions when striped bass have been reluctant to strike, and during the daylight shift it's a dependable way to catch weakfish, fluke, sea trout, redfish and occasionally snook. The combination of the clacking sound and a delicious-looking bait must be hard to pass up.

A variation of the natural-rigged shrimp, which faces the shrimp forward, is to rig the shrimp in reverse with the hook in the tail. Use the D.O.A. shrimp and remove the factory-rigged hook from the lure, reinserting it into the tail. Push it through, bending the shrimp until the hook point pops out about one third the way down the tail. To finish the lure, trim the tail fins so the shrimp won't spin on the retrieve. If you are using unrigged shrimp bodies, use the nickel-plated Eagle Claw 189 baitholder hook. You can use lead nail weights or the D.O.A. shrimp weights. This is a great rig when you need extra casting distance or when you have to punch through a strong breeze.

CAROLINA AND TEXAS RIGS

Taking a page from the freshwater bass angler's journal, rigging a shrimp body on a Z-hook is another great way to fish a fake shrimp. The weight of the hook keeps the bait suspended right-side up so it looks natural. Go deep by rigging the shrimp Texas-style with a bullet weight at the nose, or Carolina-style on an 18- to 30-inch leader.

Several hook manufacturers make Z-hooks with a lead weight molded to the shank. They are good alternatives, especially in very shallow water where fluke will aggressively grab them. D.O.A. markets a special pinch-on weight that easily presses to the shank of virtually any Z-hook.

Carolina and Texas rigs are very effective when fishing over grass beds, especially when casting to pot holes while drifting or poling. The Texas rig is also good when casting along shallow drop-offs, close to dock pilings and around sand bars. The Carolina rig is often favored in slightly deeper water.

GO DEEP WITH LEADHEADS

Fishing a shrimp body on a leadhead is a popular way to present the shrimp in deep water, and it offers dramatically improved casting performance—a valuable bonus on windy days. The angler can choose from a variety of leadhead shapes and attachment-eye positions to infinitely vary the retrieve action. Eyes on the front of the leadhead produce a less exaggerated hopping retrieve than do eyes on the top of the leadhead. When fishing vertically, the on-top position of the attachment eye produces the best action, such as when drifting along the deep edge of a marsh or channel edge, or near a bridge abutment or dock piling.

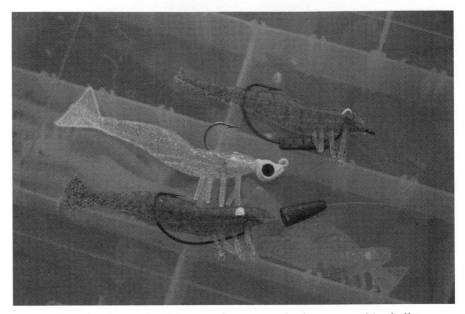

Fake shrimp can be rigged in a variety of ways to make them suspend in shallow water or go deep to plumb the depths.

When fishing a leadhead, I generally stick with a slow action and use short lifts of the rod tip to make the leadhead/shrimp combo dance seductively. Spinning tackle is generally the most popular, but you can really make a shrimp come alive when using any of the small, oval-shaped baitcasting reels specially designed for saltwater use. Bounce the lure just off the bottom and you'll be rewarded with striped bass, fluke and weaks; or snook, trout and reds.

To present the most realistic profile, if the plastic shrimp body has a rounded nose, which most do, cut or bite a small piece from the nose to form a flat surface that will butt up neatly to the back of the leadhead.

THE ULTIMATE SHRIMP

A natural-rigged shrimp with a small weight in its belly is a deadly lure when fishing in shallow water for trout and redfish, snook and striped bass, or when casting to fish that are holding high in the water, such as at night when snook and striped bass are glued to dock or bridge pilings waiting for a meal to drift their way. When you need to go deeper or when dealing with fast currents, but still keep that natural-rigged look to the shrimp, there's another rig that works well. Let's call it the ultimate shrimp because it not only adds extra weight for casting distance when fish are just out of casting range for a light-weight shrimp or to overcome windy days, plus this rigging technique adds sound to the equation. If you've ever had the chance to snorkle where there are many shrimp, you'll hear the clicking noise they make, and by adding a rattle chamber, the ultimate shrimp becomes that much more realistic. It also uses a nearly weed-less Z-hook for solid hook-ups.

I've used this rigging style in Florida for snook and trout, and in New Jersey for striped bass and weakfish with equal success. To make up a few ultimate shrimp you'll need some pre-rigged shrimp, and you'll also need 5/0 Z-hooks, pinch-on weights and rattle chambers. All the parts are available at many tackle shops or directly from D.O.A. They can easily be rigged on the boat, but it's handy to rig several ultimate shrimp ahead of time at home at the workbench so

To rig the ultimate shrimp, start with a D.O.A. replacement shrimp body (or remove the hook from a pre-rigged shrimp), rig a Z-hook from the tail end of the bait, clip the fins to avoid spinning, add a pinch-on weight and a D.O.A. belly weight, and finally add a rattle at the nose of the shrimp. This lure will cast far on a windy day and is virtually weedless. To fish shallow water, eliminate the pinch-on weight.

you don't have to waste time while on the water. If it's a hot bite, you don't want to take time away from casting and fishing to rig a lure.

Begin by removing the original factory-installed hook by pushing it rearward. It will slide free of the shrimp leaving a small channel where the hook shank used to be. Insert the pointed end of the rattle chamber into the channel where the hook used to be, and push it until the rattle is completely inside the shrimp. By working your fingers around the nose of the shrimp you can push the rattle in deep enough so the soft plastic closes around the rattle. It will not slip free during casting.

Trim the tail fins so they taper from a point at the tip of the tail, but do not remove the entire tail. This will help the lure ride true and straight with no chance of spoiling the action if the bait were to spin on the retrieve. Insert the Z-hook about ⅜ inch into the tip of the tail-end of the shrimp, then push it through until the tail is seated at the hook eye. Insert the hook point into the body of the shrimp so the point is just barely exposed along the top of the shrimp. The shrimp body should lie perfectly straight with no bend, which would cause an erratic action. Add a pinch-on weight to the hook shank and the ultimate shrimp is completed.

ANY COLOR YOU WANT

A natural live shrimp will take on the coloration of its surroundings, so it most often displays a clear, tan, brown or greenish color, often with spots. At night they can exhibit a glow from nearby dock or bridge lights. It's not surprising that some of the most successful fake shrimp colors are clear, tan, brown and fluorescent, and also those with flash foil inserts that present a holographic image, like the Tsunami shrimp.

Bright colors also attract plenty of strikes. Many northern anglers subscribe to the "If it ain't chartreuse, it ain't no use" philosophy, and there's no denying this bright green color catches plenty of fish. Its bright color vividly punches through murky, discolored or cloudy water so gamefish can home in on it and strike. It works equally well in southern waters, and I've had some excellent snook catches in Hobe Sound and in the Loxahatchee River with bright chartreuse shrimp. Pink is another popular bright, flashy color.

Going to the other extreme, the dark brown root beer colors seem to work exceptionally well in the Carolinas and Florida for snook and trout, and at night in northern waters when seeking striped bass. The dark profile imitates the shrimp's natural ability to blend in with its surroundings, and at night the dark body is silhouetted nicely against the sky making it an easy target for striped bass.

Many guides prefer the more natural-look of colors such as silver fleck and gold fleck; two colors that are nearly clear but with a hint of color that exactly imitates the coloration and visual look of a live shrimp. Another superb choice, and one of my favorites, is the glow shrimp. For some reason its fluorescent glow, even in daylight, is very appealing to sea trout, redfish, snook and many other southern gamefish. Kidding around while chumming for bonito off Jupiter (little tunny or false albacore to northerners), I had a nice, fat 12 pounder slurp down a glow shrimp. The fish was probably very surprised,

Paul Hetherington of Oakley Sunglasses took this plump trout on a shrimp using Captain Mark Bensen's "minesweeping" technique, which keeps the shrimp on the surface in very shallow water. It works!

but I wasn't. Glow shrimp have good mojo and are famous for catching all kinds of gamefish.

Shrimp baits open up many opportunities to catch your favorite gamefish. Whether you're an old hand at fishing with artificial shrimp looking for some new tricks, or just starting to fish with fake shrimp, there's no doubt about their fish-catching abilities. They are must-have lures for every tackle bag.

CRUNCHING CRABS

One thing gamefish and fishermen have in common, we love to eat crabs! Snook and bass, trout and weakfish, fluke, permit, jacks, tarpon and redfish, they all dine on crabs, from little bitty-size crabs no bigger than a dime to hand-size critters with a real nasty disposition. They are abundant and available for most of the fishing season. The blue claw is the most commonly known with its bright colors and fine-dining qualities, but there are several other olive-, brown- or tan-colored crabs, and close cousins of the swimming crab family, which are equally important as food for gamefish.

Blue claws and their less-fancy relatives spawn in coastal estu-aries from spring through fall and provide a steady diet of high-pro-tein food for gamefish. The higher tides of the new and full moons flush larger quantities of water from coastal bays, rivers and creeks making these lunar periods of great importance to fishermen looking to take advantage of potential feeding frenzies. The "plop" and "pop" sounds you hear on a summer night at the mouth of your favorite striped bass creek are not necessarily stripers chasing bay anchovies, but might be the noisy feeding of stripers slurping down tasty crabs swimming just below the surface.

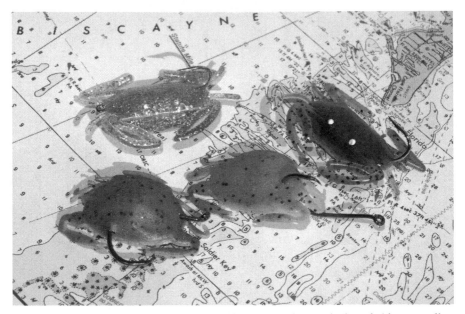

Pre-rigged or fished as a rig-your-own, a soft-plastic crab must look and ride naturally. Crabs are an essential part of most gamefish diets from Florida to Maine.

A check of the stomach contents of summer resident game fish will usually turn up a significant percentage of crabs in the diet so it makes sense for fishermen to bait up with a crab and in many local areas, fishing a live crab bait is virtually guaranteed to score a few fish for the cooler. Prior to the introduction of soft-plastic crab imita-tions, lure fishermen had no realistic alternative to the real deal.

That's all changed. The Sea Bay Crippled Crab, Riptide Realistic Crab, D.O.A. Soft Shell Crab and Berkley Gulp! Peeler Crab have all proven themselves to be excellent substitutes. These fake baits are good enough that, like artificial shrimp, many guides always carry them in their tackle bags to be ready in an instant to present a crab at the right moment.

The most popular sizes are 2 to 4 inches wide and in colors that range from realistic brown, tan and olive shades, to bright pearl white and color combos that add touches of blue and red to duplicate a live blue claw, along with Berkley's new-penny color that has been excellent for redfish on the tournament trail. Some soft-plastic crabs are weighted to sink quickly and to lie upright on the bottom, others are weightless so the angler can present baits deep, shallow or right on the surface.

Pre-rigged crabs are ready to fish right out of the package with hook and a weight in place; just tie one on and go ahead and cast. The unweighted crabs also allow rigging flexibility to use a Carolina rig, a float rig or a leadhead to match local fishing techniques. Simplicity is a key factor because many gamefish have sharp eyesight and when fishing crabs they'll thumb their nose at a big hook, a weight or a crab that just doesn't ride right. When fishing a single hook, most guides prefer to place the hook at one of the pointed edges of the carapace so the crab appears to swim naturally, which is sideways in the current. The hook can be a standard J-hook or a circle hook, which is finding favor among many Florida Keys guides.

Factory-rigged crabs inherit the benefit of the substantial knowledge and experience of their creators so they ride naturally with the

Joelle Reynolds had some fun catching this beautiful tarpon, which could not resist a life-like soft-plastic crab bait. D.O.A. Lures photo.

right balance and sink rate. Whether pre-rigged or rigged with your own favorite set up the most critical factor when fishing a soft-plastic crab is taking the time to make it look and act like a real blue claw. Blue claws don't swim like a baitfish, they have a steady, slow sideways movement driven by their flippers. There isn't much motion at all and a darting, dancing, prancing soft-plastic crab will get nothing more than a hearty laugh from a bonefish, red, trout or tarpon. A good rig will get zero hook-ups if the crab is retrieved weird.

When sight fishing, the first important consideration is to cast the soft crab ahead of the fish. Drop the lure on its head or behind the fish and the cast is wasted, the fish blasting off the flat like a U.S. Navy Blue Angels jet. If you cast too far, reel it until it's in line with the path of the cruising fish and then let the crab settle. If the fish sees the crab sink, the bait will usually be picked up. If the fish does not see it, twitch the rod once to make the crab bait dart a few inches, then let it rest again. If this got the fish's attention and it sees the bait, it should grab it and the game is on. A scented crab like the Berkley Gulp! Peeler Crab can be a big asset because fish will home in on the scent, but the most important point is to make the crab look like a real crab.

When blind casting, the rule still applies—make the crab look real. This requires extreme patience on the angler's part because we all have that natural desire to retrieve the lure, crank the handle and twitch the rod. When casting a crab, less is more, so adjust your retrieve accordingly. Make the cast, let the crab settle, then twitch it, let it settle again and wait several seconds. Repeat the twitch, settle, wait over and over until the retrieve is complete.

The minesweeping surface technique described a few pages ago for working a shrimp on the surface will also work well with crab baits. Remember that once the crab is on the surface, it does not take much retrieve speed to keep it there. It's important to close the bail as soon as the crab hits the water and make several quick reel cranks to remove slack line and get the crab up on the surface. Once the lure is up on the surface film, slow the cranking speed down, reeling with just enough speed to keep the lure making a surface wake.

When fishing around bridges where striped bass, snook and tarpon are known to hang out, make the cast as usual, but let the crab hang in the current. The natural gentle motion of the water's current will make the crab hover and look very natural. Dead sticking can also be effective, although not as satisfying because you miss the pick-up of the bait. Cast the crab, close the bail and put the rod in a holder. The current and motion of the boat is all that's needed to make the crab look good.

Artificial crabs and shrimp are favorite soft baits of guides because they're reliable and catch so many species of gamefish—like this weakfish that ate a fluorescent shrimp.

Crab baits also look natural when cast towards a rip, bar or weed line and allowed to drift with the sweep of the current. On grass flats look for sandy pot holes and fire off a cast, letting the crab sink. A twitch of the rod tip will impart a minimal amount of motion to get the attention of any fish hanging out nearby.

Like shrimp, artificial crabs are excellent baits once you master the nuances required to make them work just right. And, just like shrimp, you can leave a supply handy in your tackle bag whenever you need them so there's no need to lug around live bait.

6

THE SLUG-GO REVOLUTION

Striped bass fishermen are never content to leave well enough alone. They're always looking for a new twist, tip, technique or tactic that will give them an extra edge, catch them another fish or two. In New England, the Slug-Go bait from Lunker City has given that edge to a small group of surf and inshore fishermen. The lure is so effective, well-known surf fishermen whose names were virtually synonymous with live eel fishing, are now using Slug-Go baits instead of the real eels.

These lures, however, are not just for surf and jetty jocks, and have become popular with inshore fishermen all along the coast. Light-tackle inshore fishermen have enjoyed some terrific action the past several seasons in the fall casting 4½-inch Slug-Go baits to surface crashing albies. Rigged with a Z-hook or a light leadhead, the slender lures have become go-to baits for many guides and captains. They cast quite far on light tackle and by working the rod tip, they can be made to dance, twist and jerk with deadly effect.

The Slug-Go family of baits really comes alive in the hands of a skilled angler. While fishing with Rhode Island light-tackle guide, Jim White, I watched fascinated as Jim made a 6-inch Slug-Go come to life with twitches of the rod tip that made the lure look absolutely dazzling.

Like many fishermen, it took a while for me to get fully up to speed with fishing and rigging Slug-Go soft baits, but after a few tries a pair of stripers finally fell to a Slug-Go rigged on a Z-hook with a lead keel for some added casting weight while fishing one of my favorite bridges. I needed a lot more coaching and kept searching for more information.

Joe Farry, rep for PRADCO lures in the Northeast, showed me the big YUM Houdini Shad, which I've used to catch stripers in the Point Pleasant Canal in the spring, and also the YUM Forktail Dinger, a soft bait with a big, fat worm look that is also proving to be a winner for striped bass.

Another push toward big soft baits came at one of the Hi-Mar Striper Club's annual Fishing Flea Markets where I purchased a selection of Captain Steve's Bass Candies, a collection of 10-inch soft plastic tails with a special shape that resembles an eel. Not content to sit on its laurels, the ever innovative Lunker City crew recently introduced a new larger 12-inch Slug-Go, which is the perfect compliment to its 9-inch Slug-Go. The original 9-inch Fin-S Fish also fits into this mix of eel-like lures, plus other imitations like the Tsunami Holographic Eels, Berkley PowerBait eels and some old-time favorites that are still made by Crème and DeLong Lures. All these big soft baits are excellent striped bass foolers.

Another great soft-plastic from Captain Mike Hogan is his Hogy Lures now with new gigantic 14- and 18-inch versions of the original 7-inch and 10-inch soft baits. His hand-poured creations are unique and have a great action.

Between Lunker City, YUM, Hogy, Tsunami and Captain Steve's Lures, the wide array of sizes, shapes and colors is comprehensive; from dark to light, subdued to bright, and there's a color for every type of light and water condition. These super-size plastics work well in the surf or when cast from jetties. The super-size and mid-size versions also catch when fished along inlet sea walls, around bridges and docks, in shallow water, along the edge of marsh sedges, along rocky shores or sandy beaches, in deep inlets, over inshore lumps and on the shallow flats over eelgrass.

For some fishermen they are replacing the need for live bait. In the Point Pleasant Canal and along the channel just inside Barnegat Inlet, some fishermen believe

If you want to catch big stripers, like this one being released by Captain Terry Sullivan, try fishing a big Slug-Go, Fin-S Fish or Hogy Bait.

they are just as good as live eels. Even when bunker schools are located, a super-size plastic lure fished below the bunker on a three-way rig can still fool stripers.

They are not just a "Yankee" bait. I've used big Slug-Gos to catch snook and jacks while wading in Florida. Several guides I've spoken to have used them when sight fishing for cobia along the beaches off Jupiter and West Palm Beach, and for tarpon in the Keys. A world-record cobia ate a big eel-type bait for an angler fishing off the Florida Panhandle. Big soft baits are finding favor with boat and surf fishermen all along the coast.

There's no doubt the big plastics catch fish, but if you're a newbie just starting to use them, rigging these lures can be challenging. To make the baits fish effectively, there's a lot more required than just poking a big hook into the plastic. The choice of hook, weight and rigging style will affect the way the lure swims and how it looks to a striped bass, snook, deepwater summer flounder, cobia, tiderunner weakfish or dolphin. Only if it's rigged right will a fish eat it.

Draped with a skirt they should work well when fished off a flat line for school bluefin, little tunny or skipjack. These 7-, 9- and 10-inch soft-plastic baits are versatile and can be fished in a wide variety of fishing situations. Once you try them, and catch a few stripers on them, other tactics will probably pop into your mind. How about pulling a big plastic as the center bait on a shad rig, dropped back on a 5-foot leader? I've used the YUM Houdini Shad on shad rigs as a trailer and have been real pleased with its fish-catching ability. We've only scratched the surface with these big baits.

SINGLE-HOOK RIGS

The basic single-hook rigging methods are similar to the techniques described in Chapter 3. There are some substantial differences due to the overall large size of these baits, but some of the rigging techniques are virtually identical—just scaled up in size. The Slug-Go, Houdini Shad and Forktail Dinger are factory packaged with a single 9/0 Z-hook designed especially for these large baits. These hooks are adequate and will get the job done, especially for boat fishermen, and when rigged right, they are nearly weedless, a big advantage when there's too much lettuce in the water. The hook point, however, can be improved with a few swipes of a file. After sharpening, coat the point with a few swipes with a permanent-ink pen to add a protective coating to avoid rust. Lunker City and YUM sell packs of spare hooks and it's a good idea to have a few extras on hand. Another choice is the excellent Owner Oversize Worm Hook #5110-211. It's a huge 11/0 hook with a terrific cutting point that is super sharp right out of the package. Smaller sizes are also available but the 11/0 is an ideal choice for the big baits. The hook has an extended straight section positioned between the hook eye and where the Z-bend begins so it grabs more plastic and holds better in the big baits. The hook can be mounted so the bait is 100 percent weedless (except weed that might collect on the nose of the bait—not the hook's fault). There are other similar large Z-hooks available from Gamakatsu, Eagle Claw and Mustad.

The single-hook baits are heavy enough to be cast and fished with no weight required. The weight of the hook will make them sink slowly which is perfect for fishing shallow water, or working near bridge pilings at night where striped bass and snook hold in the shadow line. To go deeper, fish the bait on a Texas rig by sliding a small egg sinker onto the leader before tying on the hook. The egg sinker will ride on the nose of the bait and take it down deeper into the water column. Sinkers of ¼ to ½ ounce are the usual weight range. The Texas rig can be very effective.

Another good rigging choice is the Carolina rig, using a 24- to 36-inch leader. One end is attached to the hook, the other to a small barrel swivel. Before tying the swivel to the main line, slide an egg sinker in place so it rides above the swivel. This rigging system works best in deeper water and is especially effective when jigging a bait near a bridge piling, along an inlet bulkhead or deep beneath a

Big plastics can be rigged with leadheads or with single hooks. Nail weights add extra casting weight and also help you fine-tune the lure's action.

school of baitfish. With a ½-ounce weight it can be fished in 3 to 15 feet of water; with a 2-ounce egg it will reach 40 feet or more.

When casting an unweighted lure, or when rigged Texas or Carolina style, there's a wide selection of appropriate tackle. Even an un-weighted super-bait has enough mass and inherent weight to be easily cast on spinning gear or light conventional plugging tackle in bays and inlets. Since the size of the fish that may eat these baits can vary from schoolie to teen-size (or larger), a rod with a fast action and a powerful butt section is a good choice. This type rod offers good casting and plenty of power to turn decent-size fish. As a comparison reference, I use a 7-foot spinning rod and a spinning reel spooled with 30-pound braid. This outfit can turn a bass away from bridge pilings and win the argument most times, without being too heavy to fish for long periods of time.

The three-way rig is also a good choice, especially in the fall when striped bass begin to school tightly before they head south on the annual run to their wintering grounds. The YUM Houdini Shad rigged on a 24-inch leader attached to a three-way swivel above a 36-inch leader to the sinker is a very effective rig. I like bright colors, such as chartreuse and white, because these colors tend to reflect light better in the deep water of 60 to 90 feet. Use a yo-yo technique of alternately lifting and lowering the rod tip to make the lure swim and dance up and down. Since you are fishing vertically, a rod with a beefy butt and plenty of power is a good tool to lift big striped bass from the depths.

One or more insert nail weights can be added at the nose or tail to improve casting qualities, enhance the action or to go deeper. Pinch-on weights can also be added to the hook shank.

SIMPLE STINGER HOOK

The Gamakatsu Assist Hook and the Owner Dancing Stinger Hook are equipped with small loops attached to the hook shank and are a handy way to add a stinger hook at the nose of the bait. There are several variations of these two hooks marketed by Braid, FishPro and others. To make the stinger, just drape the loop of the assist hook to the eye of the main hook and you then have an additional hook at the very front end of the bait.

You can add a treble hook stinger at the bend of a Z-hook by using a small piece of small-diameter surgical tubing to keep the treble from slipping off the shank of the Z-hook while casting and retrieving. After pushing the Z-hook through the nose of the plastic bait, slide the treble hook eye onto the Z-hook shank, then slip the surge tube in place, and finally insert the Z-hook point into the bait as you would usually do to make it weedless. The treble hook rides slightly behind and below the main hook and adds plenty of extra hooking power.

LEADHEAD RIGS

Jumbo soft baits can also be fished on leadheads as described in Chapter 4. Since leadheads are available in a wide variety of head shapes and weights, a big Slug-Go-type bait can be fished at virtually any depth, or any fishing situation. Leadheads will take large soft baits down deep at inlets where the current is strong, or around docks and bridge pilings, along channel edges or the edge of a marsh sedge.

Captain Steve's Lures and Tackle also offers a special weighted leadhead that is inserted just like a regular leadhead, but since the weight is so slim, all that shows are the hook eye and the hook point. The slim profile of this leadhead lead is slid inside the big bait. The silhouette of the bait retains its slim shape with the added advantage of terrific action when the rod tip is worked up and down. It's a neat way to rig and provides a unique action that is well known by some coastal sharpies as just the ticket for fooling stripers.

The Bass Candy soft-bait hook is available in two sizes, and the lead weight is molded right onto the hook shank, with bumps at each end of the lead to grab onto the plastic and hold it in place while casting. This is the simplest rigging method when weight is needed for casting distance or to get the lure deeper. It works well in the surf and when casting from boats. The cadmium-plated hooks are improved with a few swipes of the file and then dressed with a permanent-ink pen.

DOUBLE-HOOK RIG

Using a special double-hook rig will catch short-striking bass, and bluefish that want to ruin your day. I first saw this rig at a winter fishing seminar and the hooks were snelled in place, rather than crimped, with a length of 80-pound Dacron for the ultimate in flexibility. Two months later at another show in Providence, Rhode Island, I was introduced to the Hogy Lure which uses the crimped system to attach the hooks and a specially molded plastic body with a slit in the top to accept the leader. Make your own rigs or get more info on Hogy Lures from www.hogylures.com.

The rig works perfectly and is relatively easy to make. Crimp a 3- to 4-inch length of 80-pound mono leader to two hooks—one at each end of the short leader. The accompanying picture shows how to rig the plastic bait to this double-hook rig.

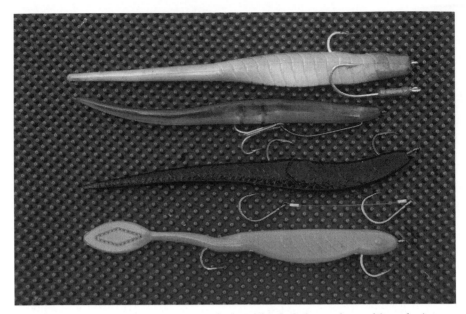

Double-hook rigs, like the Hogy rig, and stinger hooks help get the steel into the jaw of big striped bass. The Captain Steve's Bass Candy (top) leadhead is a surf and boat favorite.

The double-hook rig requires a slit in the plastic bait, such as found on the YUM Houdini Shad and the Hogy Lure. You can also use a razor blade to cut a slit of the large bait you choose a bait that does not already have a slit in it. To make the final appearance of the bait as neat as possible, seal the slit closed with super glue after the hooks are in place.

A WEIGHTY SITUATION

Adding weight is easy. Lunker City markets their pre-packaged Insert Weights 20 per bag and weighing ³⁄₃₂ ounce each. Surf anglers often push weights into the front of the bait, one on each side of the hook, and another into the tail section just aft of the hook bend. This combination seems to give added casting distance, plus an enhanced action that is very effective. The weights, however can be added in any combination that you desire to create any swimming effect you want.

If you want more convenience, stuff a few finishing nails into a small water-tight jar and use them instead of the lead inserts. Yes, they rust, but after one or two fish the lure will be "retired" anyway.

THE SURF SLUG-GO

The 9-inch Slug-Go manufactured by Lunker City started a revolution striped bass surf fishing, and the lure also works with amazing success along inshore coastal waters and bays for boat fishermen, too. The Slug-Go has been followed by a family of lures for several manufacturers that imitate the unbelievably seductive action of the original and the fame and fishing success of the Slug-Go is spreading, especially among surf fishermen, but the lure also works very well for other inshore and offshore game fish.

An early pioneer in developing rigging and fishing techniques of the Slug-Go family of baits is Steve McKenna of Rhode Island. A long-time live eel specialist well known for catching big striped bass, he switched to the Slug-Go a few years back and believes the big Slug-Go is just as good at catching stripers as a live eel, and he has the impressive catches to back it up. McKenna freely passes on his techniques and rigging methods to others, and has written about his techniques in local magazines and talks about his techniques at educational seminars.

McKenna rigs a soft-plastic bait similar to the way he rigs a natural eel. He favors Gamakatsu 7/0 Octopus hooks and 50-pound Dacron to join the hooks. When fully rigged, it weighs about 1½ ounces, casts well and sinks right into the sub-surface strike zone. To

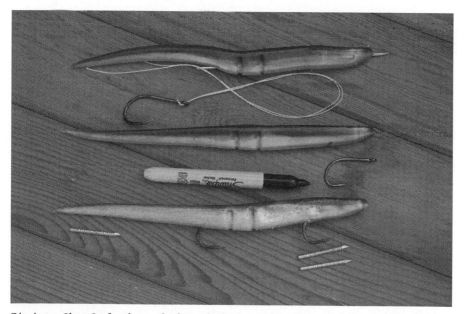

Rigging a Slug-Go for the surf takes a little time and patience, but the big-bass rewards are well worth the effort.

rig a Slug-Go you'll also need a 12-inch rigging needle, supply of Slug-Go or similar soft-plastic baits, Zap-A-Gap glue and a pack of ³⁄₃₂-ounce Lunker City insert weights.

Start by doubling over 24 inches of Dacron, then attach a 7/0 hook with a clinch knot. Thread the Dacron to the rigging needle. Starting about an inch behind the jointed section of the bait, push the needle forward until it comes out the nose. Be careful to keep the bait straight as possible and the needle in the center so it exits the Slug-Go exactly in the center of the mouth. Pull the Dacron until the hook is seated in the bait. This is the rear hook.

Next, lay the front hook along the Slug-Go body to check its position and mark the bait with a marking pen.

Push the hook point of the front hook into the bait and turn it until the hook point exits the mark you placed on the bait. The hook will push through very close to the Dacron; if you snag it, back the hook out and start again.

With the front hook in place, make sure the hooks are aligned and that the bait is perfectly straight. Pull the front of the Slug-Go back to expose the shank of the front hook. Attach the Dacron to the eye of the front hook with six half hitches and finish with an overhand knot. Trim the tag ends, then apply a few drops of Zap-A-Gap over the knots and allow the glue to dry.

To finish the lure, apply a few drops of glue, then slide the front of the lure back onto the hook shank. The glue will set quickly so work fast. Set aside to dry.

Adding weights helps the lure cast well, sink just right and maximizes its swimming action. Approximately at the bend of the front hook, insert two ³⁄₃₂ nail weights, one on each side of the hook. An optional tail weight is sometimes used to create a different swimming action, and it can pay handsomely to experiment with new ideas. After the weights are added, it's time to go fishing.

When fishing the Slug-Go, a moderate retrieve seems to work best with quick twitches of the rod. The trick is to keep the lure just below the surface at all times. The rod twitches keep the lure swimming very erratically with a side-to-side motion that stripers seem eager to investigate. You will have an easier time keeping the lure near the surface if at the beginning of the retrieve you keep the rod tip high, then lower it as the lure nears the end of the retrieve.

Although the lure somewhat resembles a natural eel, do not fish it very slowly as you would with a live eel. One essential key to the Slug-Go's success is the moderate pace of the retrieve speed. Too slow and the lure will sink, too fast and it looks unnatural; either way it loses its action and appeal.

A relatively short surf rod of 7½ to 8½ feet in length is ideal when working a Slug-Go. Too long a rod tends to impart too much action to the lure and so the 8 foot-class rods are favored. The Lamiglas XSRA-961 is a particular favorite with a nice balance of casting action and fish-fighting power.

Another reason for the Slug-Go's success is the fact that big striped bass and other gamefish come to the surf in the quiet of the night to search for food. It is to your advantage to be on the beach after the sun goes down, or before first crack of light.

There are many colors that work in the surf, but for most striped bass pros, the three favorites are black, black and black. Others will tell you that white/pearl, chartreuse, purple, root beer and rainbow trout are good second-string colors that also catch real well.

If you haven't tried the plastic big boys because you weren't sure how to rig them, I hope the preceding will get the creative juices flowing and reward you with a few more big-bass hook ups.

7

TROLLING SHADS

Trolling with shad rigs is a striper thing, and it's most popular along the mid-Atlantic and Northeast coasts. Want to catch *more* striped bass? Shad rigs are the way to go. Want to catch *big* striped bass? Shad rigs are the way to go. Okay, for sheer excitement, most striper fanatics would rather catch bass on surface poppers or deep jig them; but at season's end, a review of many a sharpie's logbook would show that, not counting back-bay fishing, more big bass were probably taken on the troll than by any other inshore method.

From April through December, trolling multi-armed umbrella rigs armed with jumbo-size, colorful soft-plastic shads do the grunt work required to catch good numbers of bass on a day-in, day-out basis. It's a technique charter skippers rely on, and one that small-boat anglers can use to score some big-time catches, too.

Even if you prefer to jig your fall stripers on heavy leadheads dressed with a soft-plastic tail, trolling with shad rigs is still an effective way to search local structure until you find concentrations of striped bass that can be jigged. And, on many days, the only consistent way to catch stripers is with a well-prepared shad rig on the troll. If you're not trolling with shad rigs, you're not even playing in the striped bass game.

Shad rigs are based upon the old umbrella rig that appeared on the scene in the late 1960s. The first umbrella rig I ever saw was on a trip to Monomoy, Cape Cod with my good friend, Captain Al Ristori. He had been fishing prototype multi-armed lures patterned after a creation made by Captain Gus Pitts, and on that trip he bagged a beautiful 53-pound striped bass—proof positive for anyone's eyes that umbrella rigs catch big fish.

Like all umbrella rigs when they first became popular, Al's rig was armed with short surgical tubes attached to the ends of each arm of the rig, and a longer tube was attached at the center.

Although heavy in weight, and with a lot of water resistance when trolled, the rigs caught striped bass like no other lure preceding them, and they quickly became a go-to lure for striped bass trollers from New England to New Jersey, and for some Chesapeake Bay sharpies. The umbrellas also caught bluefish, often several at a time, and this ability to catch multiple hook-ups gave umbrella rigs a bad rap in the eyes of some anglers. In the opinion of light-tackle fans, only "meat" fishermen used umbrella rigs.

While multiple hook-ups can be a common occurrence, there is also

IGFA rep Jeff Merrill scored this 37-pound striped bass on a shad rig trolled deep off a downrigger.

no dispute that trophy striped bass in late fall will also strike an umbrella rig, and 99 percent of the time they strike and get hooked by the trailing center lure. To savvy striped bass trollers looking for giant bass, umbrella rigs have gained a reliable reputation as a big-fish lure, and that's a good reason to make them part of your own lure arsenal.

SHAD RIG EVOLUTION

Several years ago umbrella rigs morphed into what trollers now call shad rigs. Surgical tubes gave way to soft-plastic shad bodies rigged on short mono leaders. Although shad rigs are even heavier and more resistant than traditional tube-equipped umbrella rigs, they offer several advantages, such as a wide variety of lure colors, body sizes and profiles, and swimming tails with a terrific action that seems to draw strikes better than the old-time tube rigs.

Shad rigs are amazingly lifelike in appearance and are responsible for catching large numbers of fall striped bass. You don't want to troll them when hordes of voracious bluefish are around because ol' yellow eye, those nasty bluefish, will destroy the plastic shads, but if you don't mind the occasional shredded shad, the fall is also the time to score on gorilla-size blues of 15 pounds or more.

The profile of shad bodies are spitting images of small bunker, mullet and juvenile bluefish, and their vibrating tails add the enticement of sound to the package. It is usually a great combination, but may not be as effective when slim baits, like sand eels, are present. Slender soft baits like the 7- and 9-inch Fin-S Fish and Slug-Go baits are a better choice. Although they do not have as much action, the silhouette so closely duplicates the sand eel, that striped bass will often attack these slim baits aggressively.

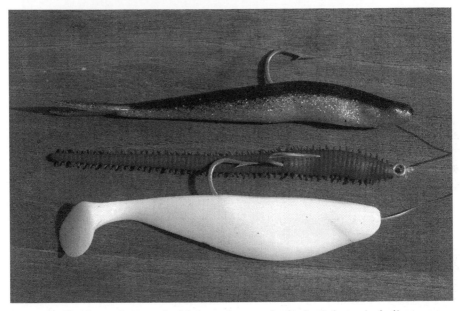

An umbrella rig can be armed with several types of soft-plastic lures, including traditional shads (bottom), imitation sandworms (center) and large jerkbaits (top).

Noted striped bass angler and writer from New England, Captain Charlie Soares, uses another excellent umbrella rig modification to fool striped bass. Charlie replaces the shads and equips some of his smaller rigs with Berkley PowerBait sandworms and relies on the combination of smell and the natural appearance of the worms to catch striped bass. His technique works and has proven effective in Long Island Sound and New Jersey waters as well.

RIG 'EM AHEAD OF TIME
For maximum hook-ups and optimum efficiency while trolling, the shads must be rigged perfectly. Your best bet is to rig up a supply of

shads ahead of time and store them in plastic bags or water-tight containers. I usually use 6-inch shads for the arms of the rig and 9-inch shads for the trailer or drop-back.

Use a long stainless-steel rigging needle inserted into the shad from the nose to pull the hook into position. This places the hook as far back in the shad body as possible and assures that the lure will track straight and true. This may seem like a small point, but it's important. If you simply twist and bend the shad body onto the hook as if you were rigging small 4-inch soft-plastic lure, the big 6- or 9-inch shad will often be slightly cockeyed, bent out of shape and the hook will be positioned far forward in the shad. Bent shads don't look realistic and won't fool wary stripers, and when the hook is far forward short-striking bass will be missed. Rig 'em right—use a rigging needle.

Rigging needles like the type I'm talking about are sold in tackle shops that cater to offshore tuna and marlin fishermen and are used to rig Spanish and cero mackerel and large trolling squids. They are typically available in 12- to 18-inch lengths and have a small notch at the end. Look for the smallest diameter needle you can find. When rigging shads you may find that the needle is very easy to insert into the shad but it is much more difficult to pull back through the shad when pulling the leader and hook into place. The soft-

Tournament Cable's rigging tool offers a handy way to rig large plastic lures, like these Tsunami shads. The hollow needle lets you push the leader through the lure without tearing the plastic. Use 60-pound mono, crimps, and 8/0 hooks to complete the shad.

plastic lure is "gooey" and tends to grab the needle. Getting a good grip on the needle can be a problem, but it's easily solved. Try bending the back end of the needle, or add a short wooden broom stick handle or dowel secured in place with epoxy glue. The handle will then be very easy to pull.

I have measured marks on the edge of my workbench so I can quickly make up a supply of shads, all with leaders of equal length and consistent uniformity. I use 80-pound mono leader because it can take a lot of abrasion abuse and tie the hook with a 4-turn improved clinch. Tie the hook to the leader, and then push the rigging needle through the bait. Insert the leader into the small notch in the rigging needle and pull the leader and hook into the shad body. A spritz of WD-40 will help the leader slide through the bait easily. After pulling the leader and hook into the bait, attach a barrel swivel via a crimped loop and you're all set to fish.

A neat alternate method uses a Tournament Cable (www.tournamentcable.com) rigging tool, which is a stainless steel hollow needle about 12 inches long. Push the needle tool through the shad bait from nose to tail. Because the needle is hollow, the mono leader is pushed through the needle until about 6 inches extends past the tail of the shad body. Tie in the hook, then pull the needle and the leader into the shad to seat the hook. Since the leader is inside the smooth needle, there's no damage to the shad, unlike in the above method, which may cause some slight tearing of the shad.

For added flash appeal, shad rigs can be rigged with small Cape Cod-style spoons at the end of each arm, and when rigged this way, the willow-leaf blades are superb striped bass attractors.

THE DROP-BACK

The trailer shad, also called the drop-back, will usually hook most bass, especially the larger fish. Rig a supply of larger shads on 24- to 48-inch leaders and store them in waterproof containers, same as you did for the regular 6-inch shads.

Other plastic lures can also be used as the drop-back, such as soft-bodied swimming plugs, big plastic squids, jumbo imitators like the Mann's Mannhaden and Williamson Lures mullet imitation, and artificial eels. One of my favorites is the Tsunami 9-inch SS9T Swim Shad in glow, dolphin or chartreuse/silver colors. Whether you arm an umbrella rig with shads, squids or life-like imitators, mono leaders are essential between the lure and the umbrella rig arm. The leaders can all be of the same length, or they can be varied so that one lure is dropped back 12 inches, another at 18, a third at 30 inches and a fourth at 36 inches. The center lure can be dropped back anywhere from 30 to 60 inches.

If you frequently change the center drop-back lure, make up the trailer leaders with snaps at both ends so they can be clipped to the lure as needed, or stored coiled in waterproof containers, plastic bags or leader bags. Remember to stretch a coiled leader before using it so it lies straight. A Duolock snap at one end clips to the lure, a barrel swivel at the other end clips to the end of the umbrella rig arm. If you want less hardware, tie the tube or shad directly to the leader, but use the same barrel swivel arrangement to snap the lure to the umbrella rig arm. Leaders for the center drop-back lure can be made up and stored in the same manner.

Here comes a trophy striped bass to the net. An umbrella rig armed with shads is a favorite lure for Northeast charter skippers and local bass sharpies.

SELECTING THE RIG

The basic wire-armed rigs are sold in several configurations, often with popular local names to describe them. They all have one thing in common, a lead weight at the center from which one or more arms sprout, much like the frame of an umbrella, hence the name— umbrella rig. The simplest rig is a straight bar, often called a coat hanger rig; the lead weight at the center has one arm projecting out on each side. The standard rig usually has four arms, but nearly as popular is the six-arm rig and there is even an eight-arm rig, nicknamed the gorilla rig by bass pros because it is so good at catching the biggest kind of striped bass.

The arms of each rig can vary in length from 12 to 24 inches, but they always have an attachment snap at the end of the arm so the shads can be clipped to the umbrella arm. Longer arms usually have a second attachment eye at the mid portion of the arm where smaller shads can also be attached. These smaller shads, if employed, are usually hookless and only serve to add to the overall mass and visual appeal of the lure—it looks just like a school of bait. Rigs with short arms are often called "mini" rigs because of their compact size. By varying the size of the rig, the size of the plastic lures and their colors, the striped bass troller can imitate a variety of baitfish schooling patterns.

Typically, shad rigs have the lures attached only at the end of the arms, not at the midway point of the arm. The shads have a lot of water resistance when towed and too many shads can make the rig very tough to handle. In extreme cases the rig will pull drag against the reel. If mid-position shads are used they are always smaller in size and attached on short leaders; about one-third the length of the leaders for the shads attached to the end of the arms. This avoids excessive tangling.

The shape and size of the center hub weight is very important. I've used many different versions of umbrella rigs over the past 40 years and have found that the torpedo or rounded shapes tend to track better than rigs with a flattened center weight, which may ride slightly cocked and at an angle. Two to 4 ounces is about the right weight for the center hub.

PROPER PRESENTATION

Getting the shad rigs down into the dining room of Mr. Bass is critical if you want to score with consistent success. There are several ways to accomplish this—a mono and drail combination, wire line, super braid line or downriggers.

The mono-and-drail trolling method works well in relatively shallow waters no deeper than 20 feet. An 8-ounce drail and a shad rig with a 2 to 4-ounce center weight will get you down about 15 feet, well within range of stripers holding on a shoal, sandy lump or sandbar. Trolling with a mono and drail combo also works well when trolling along the surf line just outside the breakers, and in shoal areas in front of inlets.

Single-strand wire is the favorite choice when fishing in 20 to 40 feet of depth. Wire takes the lure down 5 feet for every 50 feet of line in the water and is the traditional choice for anglers from New England to New Jersey, and in parts of Chesapeake Bay. With 300 feet of wire in the water, the lure will run about 30 feet deep. Add a 4- or 8-ounce drail, and you'll get another 5 to 10 feet.

Super braid is the hot new technique and it's appealing to a wider audience of striped bass trollers because it's so easy to use, and the tackle is more sporting. With its ultra-thin line diameter, 50-pound super braid slices through water like 12-pound test monofilament, so a shad rig with an 8-ounce drail will go down about 25 feet of water depth—just perfect for many of the same areas where wire line is usually employed. The beauty of using super braid is in the tackle. A typical light inshore trolling or jigging rod can be employed and the entire outfit is much lighter in physical weight, and more pleasant to use.

Downriggers are the best way to plumb extremely deep waters. Areas within the 3-mile EEZ (exclusive economic zone—that is, US waters) that exceed 40 feet are prime candidates for downrigger fishing. The ultimate hotshot lure is a shad rig with chartreuse or pearl shads. An AFTCO downrigger release clip can be adjusted with enough firmness to hold the shad rig yet it releases when a big bass strikes.

Shad-rigged umbrella rigs are usually fished down deep on wire, downriggers, or super braid to get to the most productive bottom structure.

RODDIN' AND REELIN'

Fishing from a small boat requires careful tackle selection, and choosing multi-purpose rods and reels is a big advantage. It is usually most productive to fish your trolling setups in pairs. The Lamiglas BL7030W is a superb choice for most coastal striped bass trolling. Equipped with Fuji Silicon Nitride II guides, it can be used for wire, super braid or mono. The guides are tough enough to laugh at the abrasiveness of wire, and smooth enough to handle mono and super braids with a soft touch. Carrying spare reels allows the angler to switch from wire to super braid in just a few seconds without the need to invest in another pair of rods. Start the day with a pair of Penn Senator 113H or Shimano Tekota 800 reels filled with 300 yards of wire line and keep a second pair of smaller reels, such as the Penn Torque 100 or the Tekota 500, filled with 30- or 50-pound super braid in your tackle bag. When you need to switch to downriggers or straight super braid trolling, just switch the reels.

Whether trolling with wire, super braid or mono, it's a good idea to add a length of 50- to 60-pound clear leader at the end. Wire and super braids have virtually no stretch so the leader acts as a shock absorber when a big bass smashes the rig. It's also a good handhold to haul a fish aboard, and it's less visible to the fish than the wire or super braid line.

Before tying a large snap swivel at the end of the leader, slip a big plastic bead on the leader. The bead cushions the impact if you reel the snap all the way to the rod tip and prevents busted tip-top guide rings.

DO THE MATH

Accurately calculating the trolling depth is critical to success. With single-strand wire, like Malin's pre-marked Monel wire, the calculations are easy—50 feet of line in the water gets the lure down 5 feet. For super braid, use a permanent marker every 100 feet, or tie in an 80-pound size Krok barrel swivel every 100 feet. When using a 4-ounce shad rig, for every 100 feet of super braid in the water, you'll reach about 7 feet of depth. Add an 8-ounce drail to get an additional 10 feet of depth.

Shad rigs are a great striped bass lure and enjoy a fine reputation for catching big fish.

When fishing downriggers, the scope of the trolling wire away from the boat must be taken into account. Veteran downrigger trollers add 20 percent to the trolling depth to make up for this scope. If the striped bass are marked at 25 feet, let out 30 feet of downrigger cable.

With super braid or downriggers, shad rigs can be used to catch southern species like grouper, mutton snapper, cobia and jacks.

HOUSTON, WE HAVE LIFTOFF

Getting a multi-lure shad rig into the water without tangling all the tubes or shads can be tricky unless you "launch" the rig properly. If the shad rig is simply dropped into the water, the shads will turn backward as they hit the water and tangle around the main leader, the short lure leaders or the arms of the rig itself making quite a mess. The fouled lure will not look realistic and will most likely go fishless.

To make a tangle-free launch, reel the rig to within a few inches of the rod tip, keep your thumb on the spool and engage the reel's clicker. Point the rod at a 45-degree angle away from the transom and keep the rod tip low to the water. With the boat in gear and moving forward, swing the rod tip forward in an arc so the umbrella rig moves like a pendulum and plunges into the water with shads swinging behind it. Immediately free-spool the reel and allow about 25 feet of line to stream from the spool. Stop the line with thumb pressure, and with the rod tip pointed low and at the water, take a close look at the rig to be sure no tubes or shads are tangled, and then continue to stream out line until the lure is at the proper depth.

The pendulum swing is easy to master and makes deploying an umbrella rig a very simple chore. As the lure plunges into the water, the natural resistance of the water keeps pressure on the tubes or shads so they remain tangle free. The pendulum swings works equally well with wire line, lead core, mono or braid.

Shad rigs are one of the most popular trolling lures for striped bass, and they are especially deadly on big bass in the fall. They are a must-have lure for your trolling arsenal.

8

SOFT PLASTICS OFFSHORE

Imitation squids ushered soft plastics onto the offshore stage many years ago, popularized by the charismatic Frank Johnson at Mold Craft Lures. His "rubber" squids were rigged as single baits to troll for yellowfin tuna and marlin, and as groups of squids rigged as daisy chains for giant bluefin tuna. Hatteras and Gulf coast skippers used daisy chains of large squids as hookless teasers to help entice strikes from blue marlin, while Florida captains used similar but smaller daisy chain rigs to fool sailfish.

By today's standards these early soft lures seem unsophisticated, but they got the ball rolling and are still used every season by many blue-water crews. Why not? They work, and over a million Mold Craft squids have been sold. Soft-plastic lures for offshore fishing, however, did seem to be stuck in a time warp during the 1990s, a time when innovation seemed to be on hold until the clocks ticked past K2M, but then an explosion of new soft-plastic lures designed and molded specifically for offshore pelagic species like dolphin, tuna and marlin rang in the new century. For offshore anglers the arsenal of new soft-plastic lures is awesome and still growing.

The traditional soft squids now team up with a cadre of exceptionally realistic imitations of ballyhoo, cutlass fish, skipjack, Spanish mackerel, mullet, flying and cigar minnows. With innovative rigging methods, a skilled mate can rig an artificial ballyhoo to look just about as good as a fresh, natural ballyhoo; and with the additional appeal of a wide array of color choices. There's no denying that a well-rigged, natural, silver-scaled ballyhoo looks real good in the trolling pattern, but offshore trollers are discovering there are times when a bright pink or chartreuse fake ballyhoo is also a terrific lure. Add a skirt and you've got an exceptionally good lure that needs no salt, no cooler on deck to keep it refrigerated and it's always ready for action.

Artificial ballyhoo are much more durable than the real deal. Many times you can catch more than one fish on the same lure before it has to be re-rigged. Frank Johnson displayed a billfish-battered fake ballyhoo at the Miami Boat Show several years ago. That particular lure had taken three sailfish, and despite some ugly rub marks and scars, it was still fishable!

Offshore dolphin eagerly eat jumbo versions of the same soft-plastic baits used by inshore fishermen.

Super-size, 9-inch shads originally intended for striped bass are now being trolled for dolphin, school bluefin tuna, longfin albacore, yellowfin and bigeye tuna. Just drape a skirt over the body and you have a killer lure. Huge and heavy leadheads matched to gigantic curly tails and jumbo-size tube lures are hot lures when jigging yellowfin and bluefin tuna in a chunk or a chum slick. Overgrown swimbaits like Tsunami's 9-inch, 6½-ounce SS9T Swim Shad have dual attachment eye positions so they can be jigged or trolled with equal success. Similar swimbaits from Storm look like they are on steroids and just the right size to offer a mouthful to a yellowfin tuna.

Leadheads, bucktails and swimbaits, are deadly when cast toward weedlines, floating debris or lobster pot markers where dolphin of all sizes, peanuts to bulls, hang out. Toss a handful of small cut bait as chum to get the frenzy going and you can cast soft plastics to aggressively feeding fish until your arms fall off.

Natural belly strip baits are another example of a traditional bait that has been easily duplicated in soft plastic. To make them tougher, special fabric inserts are molded into the strip to prevent tearing while trolling and to withstand attacks by sailfish and marlin. They are popular with sailfish trollers, and like the artificial ballyhoo, require no special storage, salting or refrigeration. They are very handy baits and are rigged exactly in the same manner as a fresh bonito belly strip.

SQUID DAISY CHAINS

If one lure is good, it stands to reason a string of lures should be even better. Over 40 years ago, as an observer in the Cape May Marlin and Tuna Club's annual marlin invitational, I had my first chance to see daisy chains attract not only billfish, but tuna as well. A string of soft-plastic squids was rigged to run in the wake of the *Trophy Run*, a local charter boat, but it was hookless, serving only as a teaser to help attract fish into the trolling pattern. The boat and angling crew came in second place with a beautiful 76-pound white marlin, due in part to the attraction of the squid daisy chain.

The bright pearl squids caught the interest of both marlin and tuna, the captain cursing the tuna since the only qualifying point fish in the tournament were marlin; but that daisy chain of soft-plastic squids run off an outrigger got smashed several times by billfish and tuna, and also a giant bull dolphin. Over the two days of the tournament, a total of 14 white marlin, including the second-place fish, were caught with the help of the daisy chain. Teaser daisy chains are used around the world to catch billfish and tuna; and they can be rigged in several different ways depending on whether you wish to troll them as a hooked lure, or as a hookless teaser for bait-and-switch fishing.

The hookless versions are meant strictly to tease, attract and draw the interest of billfish into the trolling pattern where they will hopefully strike a rigged ballyhoo, mullet or strip bait; or the teaser attracts the fish close to the boat, is pulled away from the fish and a pre-rigged pitch bait such as a ballyhoo or mullet is free-spooled back to the fish. Pitch baiting, also known as bait-and-switch, is an exciting way to fish offshore, with greater challenge and skill required of captain, mate and angler; but the reward for fooling a fish with a teaser and pitch bait is exceptional. Crew and angler teams experienced at this technique are at the highest level of angling achievement, at the top of the game, and a properly rigged daisy-chain teaser is often an essential component of this technique.

Plastic squids have long been used as daisy chain teasers to attract members of the tuna tribe and billfish, like this dazzling blue marlin. Rich Barrett photo.

Offshore anglers who prefer to simply troll with no bait-and-switch intentions prefer to rig a daisy chain with a hook at the tail end. Frank Johnson showed me a neat way of rigging a daisy chain of artificial squids that also offers easy storage and quick replacement of any squid damaged by a billfish attack. The squids are rigged individually on 18-inch leaders with a barrel swivel at the top end of each leader, and large snap inside the squid. A large plastic bead serves as a stopper to prevent the snap from pulling through the squid body. The squids are clipped together to make a long 15-foot chain of lures and can be disassembled when the trolling trip is over for neat storage. Most important in my mind; there was a hook at the end of the chain.

Back in the early 1980s when I first began running a Mold Craft squid chain on the third wake in my pattern, the lure quickly began to produce fish, especially bigeye tuna, and it remains one of my favorite trolling lures many years later.

Making a daisy chain is easy. Start with a 10- to 15-foot length of leader and attach a hook at the bottom end with either a snell or a crimped offshore loop. The pound test of the leader will vary; inshore small 3- and 4-inch squids for school bluefin, dolphin and little tunny are best rigged on 80- to 150-pound leader while big 6-

to 12-inch offshore squids will stand up to bigger fish and be more durable if the daisy chain is constructed on 200- to 400-pound test.

Stoppers are needed along the leader to hold the squids securely in place so they don't slide up and down the leader. Johnson, always the master at simplicity, uses ½-ounce egg sinkers crimped to the leader with pliers for quick and easy rigging. Other skippers use a plastic bead and a barrel crimp; the type with a round hole, not the oval or double crimp. The stopper should always be about ¼- to ½-inch in diameter; large enough so it does not pull through the soft squid body.

I make up daisy chains at my workbench, which has marks along its front edge every 12 inches to help with tackle and lure-rigging chores. After attaching the hook, slide the first sinker onto the leader then the first squid. The hook should be positioned at the end of the squid's tentacles. Make a visual measurement against the marks on the workbench edge, slide the squid forward of the hook, position the sinker and squash it in place with the pliers. Apply only enough crimping pressure to grip the leader without crushing, chafing or pinching the mono or fluorocarbon material excessively, which would weaken it.

Slide the next egg sinker and lure onto the leader and crimp in place about 12 to 18 inches ahead of the bottom lure. Continue until you have several squid lures on the leader. The crimp always goes on

Soft squids rigged as a single daisy chain or on a spreader bar create a massive surface commotion that catches the attention of offshore pelagics.

the leader first, then the lure. Complete the daisy chain with a crimped offshore loop knot to attach the rig to the snap at the end of your wind-on leader.

To make a hookless teaser with a daisy chain of squids, replace the bottom hook with a loop in the leader to hold the egg sinker in place. Tie a surgeon's loop at the end of the mono, or make the loop with a crimp. The egg sinker will ride against the crimp or the knot and hold the squid firmly in place while trolling. Although not as neat looking as the crimp loop, I like the surgeon's loop because it is very bulky, making it more difficult for an aggressive marlin to pull the squid from the daisy chain.

Here's an optional way to rig a swimming daisy chain that assures additional splashing action from the squids. I use a leader system that employs one long main leader and then add several short leaders at evenly spaced intervals along its length. The short leaders are crimped into place with an oval aluminum crimp or a double brass crimp with two holes looking much like a side-by-side shotgun barrel. Aluminum or brass, be sure the crimp is designed to match the pound test of the leader so you get the strongest connection.

Use a 10- to 15-foot leader and attach a hook at the bottom end, slide the first, or bottom, squid into position as described above and crimp into place. Cut several 12-inch lengths of leader of the same pound test as the main leader. Slide an oval or double crimp down the leader to a position approximately 24 inches above the bottom squid. Insert one of the short leaders into the other open slot of the double crimp and crimp the short leader to the main leader. The tag end of the short leader should be pointing to the top or forward end of the daisy chain leader.

Slide the squid mantle-end first (not the tentacle end) into position on the

This Hudson Canyon bigeye tuna was hooked on a daisy chain of multiple squids trolled on the face of the fourth wake in the center of the trolling pattern.

short leader, followed by an egg sinker or a barrel crimp-stopper bead and crimp into place. Complete the chain by attaching the remaining short leaders at regularly spaced intervals along the main leader. Add a loop at the top end of the leader and the daisy chain is all done.

At rest, the squids are facing in the "wrong" direction, but when trolled, water resistance swings the squids so they lie alongside the main leader splashing with much more motion than the in-line daisy chain where all the squids are crimped into place directly onto a single length of leader. The short leaders allow each squid to dance, wobble and splash in the trolling wake with much more freedom of movement. This added action makes the daisy chain look just like a pod of live squid darting and slip sliding from side to side.

Unlike single lures that run just below the surface and stream plumes of bubbles, squid daisy chains splatter and skip across the surface in the trolling pattern. To make them work effectively you may have to adjust the position of the lure in the trolling pattern, raise or lower the line's position on the outrigger halyard line to get the lure to maintain a steady action, or drop the trolling speed slightly. Too high a line position or too fast a trolling speed makes the squid chain jump out of the water and look unnatural. Excessive speed can also cause the squids to tear apart from excessive water pressure.

Daisy chains are usually fished on the first or second wake as a flat line lure, or on the third or fourth wakes from the outrigger. It's generally best to fish the daisy chain somewhere in the center of the pattern because it helps draw fish into the entire lure pattern. Place the chain too far back and it will often be the only lure that is bit. Fish the daisy in the middle of the pattern and multiple hook-ups will be much more common.

When fishing a squid daisy chain as a teaser with no hooks, it is usually fished off a leader line run to an eye about half way up the outrigger and then up to the fly bridge or tower, or back down to the cockpit. Depending on the size of the boat, and whether it is a fly bridge, express or center console layout, the captain or mate will haul on the teaser line to pull the bait away when a fish strikes. The marlin's attention is then turned toward another lure, bait or fly in the pattern only a few yards away—and with a hook in it.

FAKE BALLYHOO

Rigging and fishing with natural ballyhoo requires a lot of prep work; thaw, squeeze out the snot, poke out the eyes, loosen up the backbone, salt down and refrigerate. Some mates even take the extra step to "juice" the baits in a formaldehyde solution to toughen them up. Keeping them cool is essential or you will have a bunch of spoiled baits that blow out quickly when the stomach cavities tear apart after only a few minutes in the trolling pattern. On an extended trip, you may need to freeze several cases of ballyhoo to be sure you have a sufficient bait supply for the entire fishing session. This is not a problem if you own a 50 footer with a built-in freezer, ice maker and cockpit bait refrigeration, but small to mid-size off-shore boats may not have enough cold storage. Even on a one-day offshore trip, it's not unusual to go through 30 baits on a slow day and 100 or more baits when you're in on an awesome red-hot bite. There are even times when ballyhoo may be in terribly short supply at local bait dealers—no bait no fish!

Artificial ballyhoo overcome these logistical problems with grace and style, and they catch fish about as well as the natural baits, sometimes better. The earliest imitation ballyhoo baits suffered through some growing pains—they were too hard or too soft, couldn't hold a hook and tore apart too easily. That's all gone out the window, and the latest crop of soft-plastic ballyhoo are durable, and exceptionally good imitations of their fresh, natural counterparts. And, they have the supreme advantage of not requiring any refrig-eration. Rig 'em and store 'em in a tackle drawer or carry-on tackle bag until they're needed. Wow!

Several variations showing Mann's Ultimate Hoo with chin weight, hook-up position for trolling a weed line, and double-hook rig.

Several excellent ballyhoo imitations include the Tuff Hoo by Mold Craft with a beautiful, lifelike body and a molded-in action swimming tail. Mann's Ultimate Hoo with a molded-in paddle tail and the Ultimate Hoo II with a plain tail are also good choices. Both versions of the Ultimate Hoo have pockets to assist with hook placement and another pocket to accept a chin weight to rig a swimming ballyhoo. Williamson Lures takes a different approach with a unique nose construction that assists in easy rigging and backs up this feature with two extremely realistic color selections enhanced with flash-foil inserts. The Wanabe Bait Company's Chewy-Hoo helps keep the rigging process simple with an internal tunnel for hook and leader, and the Chewy-Hoo eyes can be popped out and removed just as with a natural ballyhoo bait.

Fake ballyhoo can be rigged with standard J-hooks or Circle hooks, with chin weights or without, and with single or double hook configurations. Just like a natural ballyhoo, the imposters can be rigged as surface splashers and as sub-surface swimmers. The Tuff Hoo stretches the tape to about 8 inches, about the size of what offshore trollers nickname a 12-pack ballyhoo. The Ultimate Hoo is 10 inches and the Williamson is 9½ inches. All of them can be purchased pre-rigged, unrigged and in bulk packs of 50 to 100 ballyhoo baits for professional crews that rig large numbers of ballyhoo baits for tournament and charter fishing.

Many veteran or traditional offshore crews have begun to swing over toward soft-plastic ballyhoo baits for use on daisy chains, spreader bars and dredges, which we'll talk about in a few more pages. The ultimate test is fishing a well-rigged soft-plastic bait side by side with a natural bait; you'll see that faux ballyhoo swim just as good, catch fish just as good and last far longer. Frank Johnson says sailfish will smack a Tuff Hoo bait, pop the rigger pin and chew on the bait while the angler free-spools until the hook is set. "A Tuff Hoo feels just like a natural bait," says Frank, "and fussy sailfish can't tell the difference."

Chuck Richardson, innovative head honcho at Tournament Cable, has experimented extensively with soft-plastic ballyhoo, and was among the first of the expert bait riggers to fully endorse their use. "I put in a lot of on-the-water time testing several brands before I would agree to use them in my custom rigs. I have complete confidence in them and so do many of the best offshore captains fishing from the Bahamas and Florida on up the coast to the Carolina Outer Banks and the Northeast canyons." That's a pretty impressive statement from a guy who is a well-respected natural-bait expert.

Chuck's soft-plastic ballyhoo rigs are in great demand and are sold by knowledgeable offshore tackle shops and several exclusive mail-

Rigging an imitation ballyhoo is quick and easy, as shown with Mold Craft's Tuff Hoo. Use a Tournament Cable hollow rigging needle to push through the center of the bait.

order offshore specialty houses like Melton's on the West Coast, J & M Tackle of Alabama on the Gulf Coast, and Finest Kind in Stuart, Florida.

Every Tournament Cable soft-plastic ballyhoo is rigged to tournament-winning standards with extra-strong hooks, stainless-steel spring chafing gear and quality mono or fluorocarbon leaders. "You may be fishing for white marlin, but you never know when a several-hundred-pound blue marlin will eat the bait. You have to be prepared," says Chuck. You can modify his basic rigging, however, to suit your own offshore fishing needs. The accompanying photos are based on a Mold Craft Tuff Hoo and the steps include the use of a Tournament Cable rigging tool. A standard rigging needle can also be used, but Chuck's hollow Leader Needle rigging tools are the coolest way to go. They're sold as sets for leaders up to 250-pound test and up to 500-pound test, and are perfect for rigging plastic squids, ballyhoo and mullet.

The Tournament Cable Leader Needle rigging tool makes the job go faster and eliminates any chance of the soft plastic being damaged by heavy pound-test leaders. Push the hollow needle through the bait from the nose to the hook pocket. Push the mono or fluorocarbon leader through the hollow tool until about 6 inches of the leader is exposed past the hook pocket of the ballyhoo bait. Crimp the hook onto the leader, remove the tool then slide the leader forward to seat the hook in position. This is the neatest way to rig a plastic ballyhoo. Dress the bait with a skirt, a lure head or fish as it. That's it.

When using an old-fashioned rigging needle, push the needle through the bait, starting at the nose and exiting at the molded-in hook pocket on the body being careful to keep the needle centered exactly in the bait. Fold over a 2-inch section of leader and capture it in the rigging needle eye, then pull the needle through the bait until about 6 inches of leader have exited the hook pocket. Be careful that the leader does not distort, deform or cut into the soft plastic. This is less likely to happen with 130-pound leaders, but more likely when using stiff 300-pound test leader. Draw the leader through the bait slowly, lubricate with saliva if needed, or squirt a shot of glass cleaner on the leader to make it slippery. Crimp a hook in place and pull the leader forward to seat the hook into the pocket.

SPREADER BARS

Tuna love spreader bars, and using soft baits to arm a well-rigged bar makes a lot of sense. It's the next step up from a single line of daisy chain squids, but with the added advantage that jerkbaits, mullet and ballyhoo can also be used to rig the spreader bar.

Early spreader bars were rigged with hollow plastic shell squids, but there are many other variations in use today. The possibilities include big Slug-Go jerkbaits, Hogy Lures and Houdini Shads designed for striper fishing, along with the several versions of fake ballyhoo. They are all excellent candidates to hang on a spreader bar because they have several advantages; terrific dancing action, huge color selection, they're inexpensive, easily replaced and quick to rig.

A complete spreader bar will have a long center leader and one or more flank leaders at each outboard end of the spreader bar. A few pages ago we talked about rigging a swimming squid daisy chain with separate, short leaders to the squids to gain the maximum action possible. Rigging a soft-plastic spreader bar is similar to that same technique where several short leaders are crimped into place along the main leader with the tag ends pointing forward so the leaders bend back when the rig is trolled.

The best spreader bar will have a soft bending action and are usually made of titanium. The Reel Seat in Brielle, New Jersey was the first to introduce titanium bars and they are now available from several sources. Avoid using a heavy stainless-steel bar that is too stiff because they just won't work as well with the soft-plastic lures. The

After hooking a hefty bigeye tuna at The Point off Oregon Inlet on a trolled spreader bar, the author applies plenty of power by fighting the fish stand-up style with gimbal belt and harness.

only exception is when trolling jumbo squid-rigged spreader bars for giant bluefin tuna where the heavy stainless bar is often preferred by some pros. The flexing of the softer bar brings out and enhances the action of the soft-plastic jerkbaits. Tournament Cable markets spreader bars in several sizes and flexibility ratings for small inshore bars to hefty offshore bars designed for bigeye tuna. Spreader bars have attachment loops at the ends and a center connection through which the main leader will be run. When completely rigged, each bar will then have a long main leader running down the center, and a flank leader at each outboard end.

Leaders will vary from 80- to 130-pound test for inshore school and medium bluefin tuna and dolphin bars, to 220- or 300-pound test leaders for offshore yellowfin, bigeye and albacore duties. The long center leader will typically be about 6 to 10 feet in length with a pair of flank leaders of 2 to 6 feet in length. Depending on the size (width) of the bar, two additional flank leaders may be required at the midway point on each arm of the bar. An inshore bar intended for school bluefin tuna will measure 18 to 24 inches across while an offshore bar will stretch the tape from 36 to 48 inches across.

Captain Mike Hogan of Hogy Lures has had some great success with school bluefin and yellowfin tuna with his jerkbaits rigged on a

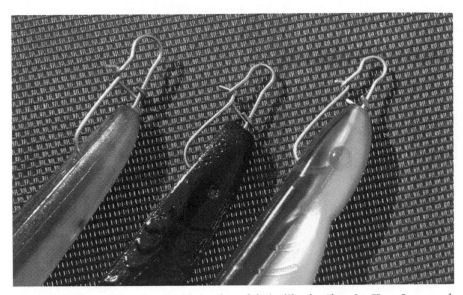

Spreader bars can be equipped with jumbo soft baits like the Slug-Go, Hogy Lure, and Yum Houdini Shad with a simple Duolock snap. Add a barrel swivel and a short mono leader for more action.

spreader bar. Captain Mike crimps short leaders into place at regular intervals about 12 to 16 inches apart along the main and flank leaders. The leaders face forward so that water pressure will bend them back while trolling. At the end of each short leader, he crimps a large Sampo Duolock snap and swivel into place. The bend of the Duolock snap is the perfect size to attach the soft-plastic baits to the leaders and they also facilitate quick replacement when a jerkbait gets torn off. Simply push the snap sideways through the nose of the bait about 3/8 inch behind the nose and you're all set.

At the business end of the main leader, a Mold Craft wide range Soft Head armed with a hook is crimped into place. This soft lure is a good compliment to the jerkbaits as they do their thing by adding plenty of action and commotion, and the Soft Head does the fish-hooking job.

An alternative rigging method uses a Duolock snap pushed into the nose of the bait directly from the front. Start by pushing the snap into the bait sideways into the nose until the wire of the snap penetrates the soft plastic, then push the snap straight into the bait about a half inch. Bend the bait so the snap exits at the top of the head. Close the snap and you're ready to fish.

Soft-plastic rigged spreader bars can be trolled within a range of 4 to 6 knots, which is the same ideal trolling speed for split-tail mullet and swimming ballyhoo. The bars provide plenty of splash, action, commotion and surface disturbance to attract the attention of tuna, dolphin and, at times, billfish into the trolling pattern and the natural baits and the soft-plastic baits enhance the fish-catching abilities of each other and make a great combination.

DREDGES

For the past several years, dredges have been the hot ticket used by tournament-winning sailfish crews power drifting off the Florida coast along the deep drop. Lowered below the boat on a heavy leader and a short, stout rod and reel combo, the dredge with its numerous baits looks like a bait ball suspended below the shadow of the hull, and it can be raised or lowered as needed. A dredge is the ultimate culmination of daisy chain and spreader bar technology combined into a giant, super-size teaser.

A substantial difference, aside from its huge size, is that a dredge always runs beneath the surface of the water where it is not as easily visible as is a surface-running teaser or spreader bar. The crew must be able to see the dredge to verify it is running properly and that gamefish haven't plucked a few baits from the arms of the dredge.

Opinions vary, but most crews work the dredges somewhere between the first and third wakes, always keeping the dredge fairly close to the boat.

The first dredges were rigged with fresh, natural ballyhoo or mullet and took the mate and crew a lot of time to rig for a day's fishing. At day's end, the baits would be chucked, and tomorrow a new set of baits rigged for the dredge teaser. Using soft-plastic ballyhoo, mullet, bunker and mackerel imitations saves a lot of rigging time, and at the end of the day, the imitation rig can be stored in a bucket or special bag and be ready for

A dredge fished below the surface looks like a bait ball and attracts offshore gamefish to investigate. The author caught this sailfish off Key West.

fishing the next day, or next week, within a few seconds. Gone are the added hours of time to rig all those natural baits.

It didn't take long for dredges to show up along other parts of the East Coast and in the Bahamas and Mexico to help fool wary sails, and marlin too. Although bulky, the latest variations of dredges can be trolled at speeds up to 4 knots or more.

If you are not familiar with them, dredges are like huge umbrella rigs, and are usually stacked one rig on top of another spaced about 2 feet apart and connected to one another by short lengths of heavy monofilament. The largest dredges usually place a 48-inch arm at the top of the rig, then a 36-inch rig followed by one or more 24-inch rigs to create the best illusion. The end result is a series of rigs, draped with dozens of baits that when strung together give an Oscar-winning performance of a huge ball of bait—something sure to get the attention of nearby billfish.

Many experienced offshore and sailfish crews build their dredges from standard fare striped bass umbrella rigs; the same rigs we talked about in chapter seven, and they favor those rigs with a heavy wire frame with a lead weight at the center. These rigs work fine for some applications, but if you use dredges a lot, stick with the heavy-duty rigs made especially for this type of fishing.

A step further along the evolutionary trail is Tournament Cable's Technical Rigs with their titanium arms for greater flexibility and enhanced action. They come in two versions; a fixed-arm type and a collapsible type that is beautifully made and offers quick, easy storage.

Since the dredge is a giant teaser, there are no hooks in it. It is heavy and is trolled well below the surface of the top-water baits or lures in the trolling pattern. Many crews will use plastic baits on the inside of the rig, and still use naturals on the outside ends of the arms.

When dredges are used power drifting for sailfish along a deep edge of bottom structure, a temperature break, water color change, weed line or rip line where two opposing currents clashed, the weight of the dredge need only be sufficient to keep it stable in the water as the boat is bumped in and out of gear to maintain a steady fishing position. When power drifting, the speed of the boat relative to the water and current is relatively slow, although the current may make the boat seem like it is moving at twice that speed relative to the bottom.

When trolling, the weight of the dredge is much more important because the boat is moving, relative to the water, at speeds up to 4 knots or more. Two factors come into play; the weight of the dredge and the resistance of the baits in the water. Water pressure exerts

Here's a close-up detail showing how to rig a fake ballyhoo on a dredge. Tip: *Dredges have a lot of drag in the water. Notch the tail of the ballyhoo to relieve the pressure so the tails don't vibrate right off the lure.*

Dredges resemble a bait ball, and they're available in a wide array of sizes for boats small and large, for power drifting, and trolling. The largest dredges stack several arms together to imitate a massive bait ball.

drag on the baits, which will cause the dredge to lift at trolling speeds. The dredge must have enough weight to maintain its position below the surface of the water despite the drag of the baits. Additional weight can be added by clipping heavy trolling drails or torpedo weights at the top end of the dredge to help keep it below the surface. Instead of a heavy weight, use a jumbo-size Mann's Giganticus 50+ deep diver lure to keep the dredge down deep.

Water resistance can be powerful and some soft-plastic baits will have more drag than others, especially those with large paddle tails. To overcome this, the tails can be split with a knife, or cut with a vee notch, to reduce the water drag factor. In extreme cases, too much trolling speed will literally wiggle the tails right off the baits.

JUMBO SHADS, LEADHEADS AND SWIMBAITS

In a previous chapter we talked about fishing leadheads and bucktails, and their swim-bait close cousins for back-bay and inshore fishing. Giant versions of these lures can also be fished with great success in the offshore blue water for pelagics like tuna and dolphin.

Just to have some outlandish fun, a charter customer of mine rigged a huge 18-inch rubber worm on an 8-ounce arrowhead bucktail. He lived in Pennsylvania and liked freshwater largemouth bass tournament fishing, and used this huge worm as a prank when fishing with a new tournament partner. At the appropriate time he'd pull the big worm from his tackle bag saying, "I hear the bass are pretty big in this lake so I came prepared!" The astonished look on his partner's face was always good for a few laughs. If I remember right, he found the big worm at a sports show where it was being sold as a gag lure to attract attention to the exhibitor's display of soft-plastic lures.

One night on a tuna-chunking trip at the Lindenkohl Canyon, he pulled the jumbo worm out of his duffel bag and got a good laugh from everyone onboard. The tables were quickly turned when my mate said, "Let's drop that baby in the slick and see what eats it!" My customer was up for the challenge and was soon jigging the worm and bucktail about 100 feet below the boat. It took awhile but a 60-pound yellowfin ate it, and before the sun popped out of the horizon, two more tuna and fat bull dolphin also dined on the big worm.

Many other offshore fishermen have become believers in the fish-catching powers of big soft-plastic baits in the chunk slick, and there are numerous heavy leadheads and bucktails that can be used to make a big bait plunge to the depths. A favorite bait is Berkley's 8-inch Power Grub, a curly tail plastic lure in their PowerBait series with plenty of smell and in several bright colors, such as pink, chartreuse and pearl that consistently attract tuna. Fake ballyhoo bodies, eel bodies, squids and jumbo-size jerkbaits and tube baits are all eager candidates for blue-water fishing when draped on a heavy leadhead or bucktail. Tsunami, Storm and others also market giant swimbaits of 9 inches or more in length weighing several ounces— tuna snacks for sure.

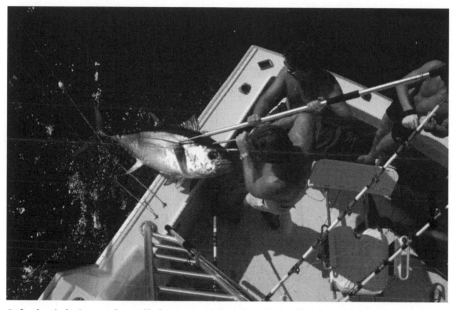

Soft-plastic baits can be trolled, cast, and jigged to fool yellowfin, blackfin and bluefin tuna; albacore and dolphin; and bigeye tuna like this bad boy about to hit the deck.

Tuna jigging has been popular off the New Jersey and California coasts since the late 1950s. In Jersey, it was school bluefin tuna that were the primary target for boats running out of Brielle, Barnegat and Atlantic City. On the West Coast, anglers were casting lead or aluminum jigs for big yellowfin, albacore and wahoo and the technique became known as "slinging iron." For bluefin, once the first fish was hooked on a trolled cedar plug, spoon or feather jig, at the strike the skipper would then ease back on the throttle, and turn the wheel so the boat made a slow circle around the school of fish. As the first fish was battled, a second angler would toss a jig into the wake, let it settle and then begin jigging the rod to make the lure dance erratically. The strikes were jolting, especially when the fish were in the 30- to 50-pound range, and the catches in terms of sheer numbers of tuna were outstanding. This technique also works just as well today, but you can use a leadhead with a soft-plastic tail in place of the metal jig and it catches inshore tuna and canyon yellowfin and bigeye.

Like the Boy Scouts, it pays to be prepared. The old-time technique just described works just fine today—if you are rigged and ready for instant action. When heading offshore, have a jigging outfit ready to go to work at a moment's notice. While trolling, after a fish is hooked up and as the boat slows, you can sometimes "buy" another yellowfin, bluefin or longfin by dropping a leadhead jig rigged with a soft-plastic tail down and into the wake. You can do this by either making a lob cast into the wake and letting the lure fall back toward the hooked fish, or by letting the jig drop well below the boat in hopes of fooling a fish that is below the surface. The leadhead can be worked in either of two ways, by jigging the rod tip and not cranking the reel to retrieve line, or be speed squidding the lure back to the boat, then dropping it back down to the depths again.

This technique takes some coordination between captain, mate and crew, but it can pay off in big dividends with a tuna or three during the day's canyon trip. Be careful to avoid getting tangled up while lines are being retrieved while clearing the cockpit.

Deep jigging, however, is the more common way to fish with soft plastic swimbaits or leadheads and bucktails. When chunking at anchor or drifting, one of the simplest ways to jig tuna is to clip the line into an outrigger clip after dropping the jig down about 50 to 100 feet. Run the rigger clip up the halyard line and push the reel's Strike lever forward so there is slight drag tension on the spool. The natural rocking motion of the boat makes the leadhead and plastic tail dance and flutter very nicely.

Deep jigging is very effective when tuna can be seen on the colorscope holding 10 to 15 fathoms below the boat, but not rising into the chum slick. Depending upon the strength of the current, drop a 6- to 12-ounce leadhead down to the feeding level of the fish. Crank the reel handle 15 to 20 times, then free spool and drop the leadhead back down. This crank-and-drop, crank-and-drop action will usually stimulate strikes. Or, some anglers just sweep the rod tip up and down to make the leadhead flash, dance and wobble. With this technique, the rod tip is pointed at the water, the angler stands sideways to the water and grabs the rod with one hand on the butt the other on the fore grip. The rod tip is quickly raised to nearly vertical, then lowered to point at the water again. This up-and-down action can be a killer technique at times.

Another effective technique is based upon the traditional drop-it-down, reel-it-in technique, which can work well when the fish are marked at random depths, but if the fish are being marked at narrow specific depth, it pays to get the lure to that exact depth. When there

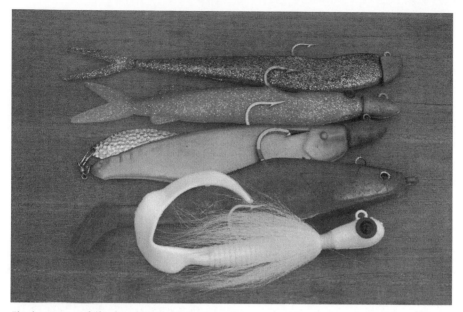

Jigging tuna while chunking with butterfish or peanut bunker can be exciting with wild, arm-jolting strikes. Heavy leadheads and big tails will do the trick.

is slow current, the jig will descend quickly and will actually appear on the colorscope so you know exactly how deep it is and if it matches the depth of the fish. With a fast current, the leadhead or bucktail will scope out at an angle and won't be seen on the scope. You have to count hand pulls or pre-mark the line with a permanent-ink pen to keep track of how much line is out.

When working a chum slick, a leadhead can also be cast out and away from the boat and allowed to settle down below the surface slick, then retrieved with either a fast and steady retrieve, or with sweeps of the rod tip. Yellowfin may be holding way back away from the boat, never coming in close enough to take your hook baits but they will take a soft-plastic lure.

The most effective way to fish leadheads is with tackle dedicated to the job at hand, rather than just clipping a jig to a standard trolling outfit. Your trolling rods and reels will probably have heavy leaders and heavy line, both of which have a lot of resistance in the water, which will inhibit the drop down of the lure and its action. Your best bet is to use small-diameter high-strength super-braid line, a high-speed reel made from the get-go to handle super-braid lines and a rod that has plenty of lifting power.

Selecting and rigging a rod and reel dedicated only to tuna jigging is relatively easy to do with the current crop of rod and reel choices.

The latest small, powerful reels from Accurate, Daiwa, Okuma, Penn and Shimano can hold a generous supply of 65- or 80-pound super braid and deliver from 30 to nearly 50 pounds of drag. That's as much drag as a big 80-wide trolling reel but at a fraction of the weight. Many East Coast fishermen, particularly party boat tuna fishermen, still struggle with the idea that huge tackle is required to fight big fish. A powerful drag and strong reel is required, but the reel does not have to be enormous. Tackle manufacturers now deliver these features in small packages that are definitely up to the task of battling big tuna. Check out the Shimano Torsa and the Penn Torque—they are beautiful, strong and worth every penny.

Jack Nilsen of Accurate Reels fights a billfish stand-up-style with one of his rugged spinning reels. Spinning gear is gaining popularity with many offshore soft-bait anglers.

Spinning reels are also an option. Check out Accurate's TwinSpin 30, which has been used to catch yellowfin and blue marlin in excess of 200 pounds, the VanStaal 300, Daiwa Saltiga and Shimano Stella spinning reels. They are rugged and dependable, and excellent choices for big game fishing.

Whatever reel you decide upon, fill it with 50-, 65- or 80-pound super line and pack it tight. On party boats you may do better with 80-pound but on charter or private boats you can go lighter and choose 50- or 65-pound test. Fill the spool to within ¼ inch of the lip so there's enough room to attach a 25-foot wind-on leader of 80- to 130-pound fluorocarbon or mono. Some anglers using conventional gear will go to a longer, heavier pound-test top-shot of mono or fluoro thinking they gain more power. While it's true that once a few coils of line are on the reel more pressure can be applied to lift the fish, the longer leader comes at the cost of slightly reduced line capacity.

Super-braid line is ultra thin and when making a loop-to-loop connection it can cut thru the Dacron loop on the end of the wind-on leader. To avoid this, I make the loop in the super braid with a Bimini of about 2-feet in length. Before tying it, thread a 1-inch piece of 80-pound Dacron onto the super braid. Once the Bimini is tied in the super line, the Dacron is trapped in the loop and is slid into position so it forms a soft cushion that protects the wind-on loop on the leader from being cut.

An alternative connection is the Albright knot, and I've also heard of some anglers using a five- or seven-turn surgeons knot to join the doubled super braid and fluorocarbon leader. Attach the leadhead directly to the leader with a four-turn clinch knot, or crimp it into place.

9

TACKLE CHOICES
THAT WORK

In these pages we've covered fishing with soft-plastic lures for back-bay light-tackle fishing, inshore coastal fishing and offshore jigging and trolling, and along the way have made some tackle recommendations that seemed appropriate to the type of lure or style of fishing being discussed. To make tackle recommendations for every type of fishing opportunity, especially for offshore fishing, goes beyond the scope of this book. A brief overview, however, of tackle tips, rods and reels, line choices along with knots and leaders, and some fish-fighting tactics may be interesting and helpful.

There's never been such a wide selection of tackle available, and depending on your viewpoint, it's a blessing or a curse that manufacturers make such an array of tackle. The choices are mind boggling, but for the tackle junky the chance to add another, and another, and another rod and reel to the arsenal is tempting. The search for the ultimate rod and reel is a never ending journey with many pleasant stops along the way to try out new innovations, the latest reel and the next "perfect" rod design.

If you are less interested in collecting lots of tackle, the selection of a limited number of rods and reels becomes more challenging and much more important; the right choice will help you catch a few more fish, the wrong choice will minimize your chances at success.

There are many factors that influence the selection of a rod and reel combination; water conditions, size of the fish, type and size of the lure, deep or shallow, strong currents and where you fish. For instance, small fish but strong currents may require heavy tackle. You may want to target schoolie stripers, but the potential to catch bigger fish must be considered. As an example, I was enjoying a pre-dawn tide with lots of action and strikes from 3- to 5-pound school stripers when a much bigger bass ate my jerkbait. On 6-pound test line and a very strong current, it took a long time to boat the fish, a thoroughly exhausted 36-inch bass I guessed at about 20 pounds. The striped bass and I would have been better served had I used 12-pound line or heavier, a beefier rod and a bit more drag. The bass would have been in better physical condition for its release and I would have had more fun fighting a fish where I could feel every head shake and lunge. On the very light tackle, the drag simply slipped, there was no sensation of a hard, tough, slug-it-out fight.

ROD ACTION

To some folks, choosing the best rod action is a black art; something mysterious and not well understood. They're probably right! One manufacturer's fast action seems to be another's moderate action, a "fast" tip can be slightly fast are really fast, and a heavy action for one company is another's medium action. Whew, how do we wade through all that?

Adding to the dilemma are the opinions of the fishermen who use the rods. I've had anglers on my charter boat who swore by a rod they said was the ultimate jigging (or casting, trolling, popping) stick, yet in my opinion the rod was mere junk. Not wanting to offend them, I kept my two cents to myself, but I also chuckled as I wondered if they may have looked at my stuff and said to themselves, "Does this guy know anything about fishing tackle?"

For most inshore fishing, a medium-action rod with plenty of power in the lower butt section and a sensitive tip is just perfect for fishing soft-plastic baits.

We all have opinions about the qualities that make an "ideal" fishing rod, but I tend to trust the opinions of guides, captains and local pros because they have the most on-the-water experience. So what do they look for in a rod?

Casting ability is high on the list followed by the ability of the rod to fight a fish with a degree of sportiness and in a relatively short time so the fish is healthy upon release. Sensitivity to feel hits and strikes, and the nuances of the lure's motion as it is retrieved are also important. So is angler comfort; a rod that feels out of balance at the start of the day will feel a lot worse three hours later. For most fishermen, a medium-action, fast-taper rod will usually fill these requirements.

The rod can only do its casting job if stressed (bent) far enough so it can spring back to its unstressed (unbent) position, thereby propelling the lure. It can only provide power to fight the fish when the rod is allowed to bend against the pull of that fish. A medium-action, fast-taper rod will usually bend progressively down into the butt section when stressed from fighting a fish or when casting a lure. Most of the bend occurs in the upper one third of the blank, and as the lure weight or the fish-fighting stress increases, the rod bends further down its length into the mid section, and finally bends into the butt section only when maximum fish-fighting power is exerted.

When choosing a rod for fishing with soft-plastic baits, you not only have to match it to the appropriate size reel to which it feels balanced, but also to the pound test of the line and weight of the lure. A rod designed for 12- to 20-pound test line and ½ to ¾-ounce lures will be a poor choice if you fish with 8-pound line and ¼-ounce lures because it will never bend enough to do the job for which it was intended. Likewise, that same rod will be overpowered if matched to 30-pound line and 2-ounce lures.

Besides balancing the rod to the fishing reel, line pound test and lure weight, the angler must also dial in some additional info about how the rod will be used; casting only, deep jigging, shallow water or deep water, or for a variety of fishing situations. For instance if you chuck soft lures at fish holding near bridges, you have to be sure the rod has enough muscle to haul a fish away from barnacle-encrusted pilings. Unlike fishing in open shallow water with no obstructions, you must have control of the fish when fishing bridges, so you need a rod with a beefy butt section. On shallow water flats with no rocks or stumps in the way, the fish can be allowed to run against the drag.

The right rod will help the action of many soft-plastic baits, such as a leadhead or swimbait. A light-action rod with a weepy tip action will not provide enough dancing and motion to the lure's action to be effective so a rod with a medium action is usually preferred.

The rod must have the power to accomplish many chores. Power, to most guide's way of thinking, translates into a rod with plenty of muscle in the lower half of the rod and a sensitive tip. The medium-action, fast taper blank is usually a great choice.

GO "LIGHT" WITH SPINNING TACKLE

Many anglers consider spinning gear to be "light" tackle because it balances well in the hand, is easy to cast and provides optimum casting distance. It's generally the most popular tackle choice with the majority of saltwater coastal fishermen. While it's easy to learn the basic casting skills, Lefty Kreh, world famous as the dean of salt-water fly fishermen and an innovative light-tackle angler, believes it takes more skill to become a master spin fisherman than it does to become a fly caster. Concentration, timing, depth of field perception and practice, practice and more practice is required to consistently plop a soft-plastic lure under a dock or overhanging mangroves, or inches from a bridge piling or boulder. No matter your skill level, however, spinning tackle is fun to use.

Today's reels offer dramatic improvements over what was available 10 years ago. As fine-diameter braided super lines became the top choice for many anglers, reel designers had to make better, stronger and more durable products. Small spinning reels originally engineered to handle 8-pound mono were destroyed when filled with a braided line having the same line diameter as the mono but testing three times the strength. Blown up spools, fried drags, wrecked ball and roller bearings, and stripped gear systems were the penalties for asking too much from a fishing tool built for lighter work.

Spinning tackle is a popular choice among light-tackle anglers and surfcasters who need versatility to cast to surface fish or to present a jighead just inches off the bottom structure.
D. J. Muller photo.

That all changed in a relatively short time. Back at the drawing board, designers came up with all-metal, light-weight body housings, rotors, spools and side plates with beefed up gear systems and husky bearings that proved far superior to their forerunners. The new drags are also impressive, fade free and smooth, and with a broader range of settings from light to heavy.

We dream of the big ones, but most of the fish any of us catch on a day-to-day basis are far from trophy catches, so fishing with spinning tackle makes the catching of these fish a lot more fun. Spinning tackle will leave you dazzled by bull-dog fights from school stripers and exciting leaps from southern tarpon. Heck, even a 3-pound bluefish will do a pretty fair imitation of a cross-country track star when caught in shallow water, and a 10-pound snook will surprise you with strong, zippy runs as it argues its case to stay as far from you as possible. Fishing with 6- or 8-pound test tackle on the flats and 6- to 12-pound gear for the rest of your inshore fishing is much more challenging than heavier gear, and it makes you think about knots, drags, lines and lures, and about your fishing skills.

Some light-tackle sharpies use 2- and 4-pound test tackle, but for most of us that's just stunt fishing. Such extremely light gear leaves the fish exhausted and the angler is totally disengaged from the fish. The drag is set so light that there's no fish action to feel, no hard yanks on the line and no sense of the battle. In the hands of an experienced angler, 4-pound test is about as light as you can go for back-bay fishing, while 8-pound is about the minimum for action outside the inlet.

Besides the dulled fight, there is also the health of the fish to consider. Catching a 15-pound little tunny on 4-pound test is very do-able, but if you want to release a healthy fish, light tackle fishing must blend sport with practicality.

BAITCASTING TACKLE

Baitcasting reels were available well before the War for Southern Independence was fought, and were generally known as Kentucky bass fishing reels. The Ambassadeur 5000 is generally credited with popularizing modern baitcasting reels in the 1960s, and the reel was so successful, variations of it are still being marketed today. Talk about popular!

The latest variations of the traditional baitcasting reel are the low-profile egg-shape baitcasting reels, seconded by the small diameter round reels so much in favor with freshwater bass anglers. They're hot for casting, comfortable to fish with and light in weight. Best of all, their built-in casting controls allow anyone to quickly master the art of casting with a level-wind reel. Click the reel into free spool, and with a flick of the wrist you can zip a soft bait to waiting weakfish, bluefish, fluke or school striper with little worries of a backlash.

Baitcasting reels are noted for their ability to plop a lure or bait within inches of the target. With minimal practice, most anglers get the hang of using their thumb to control the speed of the spool's rotation, and to stop the spool at the precise moment the lure hits the water. Casting accuracy is critical when school stripers or weakfish are holding close to the edge of a sod bank, or when a snook is up tight to a bridge abutment or holding under a dock. Baitcasting reels allow the

Need more power? Light conventional tackle is a great choice when you need that extra punch to turn fast-running gamefish, like this albie caught by marine artist Steve Goione, or to turn fish away from docks, bridges, and rocky shorelines.

angler to make casts that drop the lure literally right into the dining room where fish feed. Being close only counts in horseshoes, to catch fish that are so tight to structure, you need to be right on target.

The uncertainty of learning line control techniques is why many fishermen shy away from trying baitcasting reels. They're worried about backlashes, or spool over-runs which can cause horrible tangles. It's true that the best casters develop an educated thumb to apply slight pressure to the spool as it spins during the cast to prevent over-runs, but there are some built-in casting controls that will help first-timers.

The low-profile shape is extremely comfortable for fishing. After the cast, a right-hander would transfer the rod and reel to the left hand, palming the reel in the hand, and cranking with the right hand. By palming the reel, the angler can manipulate the rod and reel to achieve a variety of effective retrieves that can make a bucktail dance like it's alive. All it takes is a little wrist action and the bucktail can be hopped, jigged, worked erratically or tugged with gentle twitches to attract strikes.

UNTANGLING MONOFILAMENT CHOICES

In the "good ol' days," there were only a handful of manufacturers and line colors were few—clear, pink or pale blue. Today there are over a dozen line manufacturers offering a parade of choices—thin, low-stretch, hi-vis, low-vis, slick cast, extra strong, tough and soft. Taking the time to select the right line will absolutely deliver more strikes and hook-ups. It's a sure bet.

Fishermen usually say they need a line that is strong, casts well, ties good knots, lasts a long time and won't fray. Hmmmm, sounds like we want everything, doesn't it? Actually manufacturers can deliver all these attributes, and that's why they offer such a wide range of lines—to satisfy everyone.

Although the basic manufacturing process has not changed, line formulas have become more sophisticated. By changing the chemical formulas, manufacturers "dial in" precise amounts of stretch, suppleness, abrasion resistance, knot strength and casting ability to suit an infinite variety of fishing situations.

Many offshore anglers spool up with a super-braid line for maximum spool capacity, followed by a top shot of monofilament line for enhanced line handling when the fish is brought to gaff.

Fluorocarbon is the latest development in mono line. Its hard finish is extremely abrasion resistant and the line is nearly invisible in the water. Although a tad stiffer than regular nylon mono lines, new formulations are being developed to make them softer and with better casting abilities.

Choosing a line is a battle between contrasting line qualities, fishing conditions, tackle choices and where you fish. It's not always a black and white choice, and anglers must balance all these factors to select a line that is ideal for their fishing purposes.

A spin fisherman will usually achieve better casting distance with a line that is slightly stiffer rather than with a soft line, which is often preferred by a conventional bait caster. Stiffer lines are generally more abrasion resistant than softer lines, and softer lines generally tie better knots, although today's lines have come a long way to overcome this by designing special multi-polymer formulas and applying special coatings.

Mono lines stretch 20 percent or more before they break. A little stretch is good insurance against losing a trophy fish at boat side, but too much stretch makes the line act like a rubber band and this dampens the line's sensitivity.

Above all, don't be a cheapskate. Line is the least expensive part of our tackle. Why skimp on a few bucks after plopping down $100 to $300 for a top-of-the-line rod and reel combo? Heck, the fuel you burned in your car or boat to get you to your favorite fishing spot costs more than a spool of line.

The line is the direct link to the fish and the cheapest insurance policy against break-offs is to replace line frequently. It's a good idea to change your line at least at the beginning of the season, and probably once or twice during the season if you fish frequently.

MAX OUT WITH SUPER BRAIDS

What fiber is 10 times tougher than steel, yet soft as a baby's butt? The answer is super-braid fibers. Based on a fiber called gel-spun polyethylene, and trademarked under the names of Dyneema and Spectra, this is real space-age stuff. Measured in pounds per square inch, Dyneema and Spectra are much stronger than steel. That's why they're used in space ships and airplanes—lightweight, huge strength benefits.

If you've seen cotton candy being made at the seashore, you've had a peek into how super-braid lines are manufactured. Solid pellets of polyethylene are melted, spun at high speed on spinnerets which spin off a micro-fiber much like a spider's web or cotton candy. The micro fibers are then braided into a fine-diameter, super-strong fishing line.

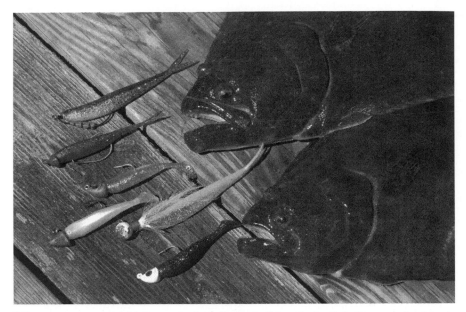

When extreme sensitivity is required to effectively fish soft-plastic baits, super braid gets the nod. Its minimal stretch makes for a line that transmits every vibration of the lure, every bottom bounce and every strike of a gamefish.

Because of their fine diameter, braids are much stronger than comparable-diameter monofilament lines. For example, 30-pound test braid has the diameter of 8-pound test monofilament, and 15-pound braid is similar to 4-pound test mono. This dramatic difference in pound-test ratings creates amazing opportunities in fishing tackle design. To take advantage of braid's extreme strength and small line diameter, manufacturers are designing smaller, lighter reels, with no sacrifice in strength or durability.

A fine-diameter line cuts through the water better than a thick line, and every reel gets a boost in line capacity because it holds more yards of fine diameter line. Small-diameter lines generally cast farther and they have minimal stretch, usually only 5 percent. That's what makes braid lines extremely sensitive. The lack of stretch also enhances your hook-setting power.

Nothing is perfect, and super-braid lines are not the be-all, end-all fishing line for every situation. The small diameter and slippery surface of braided lines makes tying some knots tricky. Braids are soft and limp, and at times can become tip-wrapped around the rod tip guide—big problem if a giant striper eats a swimbait at that same moment you're clearing a tip wrap. Line twists, conventional reel backlashes and snarls with spinning tackle are aggravated because the fine diameter, limp line is hard to pick at when trying to free a line tangle.

Super-braid lines made from Spectra fibers are woven with enhancers that make them hold their round shape and retain a certain stiffness, which minimizes the casting, handling and wind-knot problems. Lines made from Dyneema, which is slightly stiffer, need no enhancers, and some manufacturers, like Sufix, use special weaving technology that assures a round, firm line that casts beautifully. With just a little care and thought on the angler's part, fishing with super braids can be a huge improvement over mono lines, and most professional guides swear by it.

Casting With Super Braid

Mark Nichols of D.O.A. Lures is a goodwill ambassador and firm believer in braided lines, usually fishing 10- to 20-pound Power Pro with diameters approximately equivalent to 2- and 6-pound test mono, and offers the following suggestions for no-tangle line handling.

UNDER FILL THE SPOOL: Since braids are about one-third the diameter of comparable mono lines, there's no need to fill the reel to the brim. The line's slippery surface and fine diameter will enhance casting distance so the slight under filling of the spool will not reduce casting range.

CLOSE THE BAIL MANUALLY: According to Mark, a lot of line snarls, or loose coils, are caused at the instant the bail is closed automatically when the angler starts to crank the reel handle. A small coil of line wound beneath several loose coils of line before retrieve tension is applied by the lure's resistance in the water can cause a major snarl on the next cast. By closing the bail manually there is no loose line.

MONITOR THE LINE: With light lures and a jigging action, or when casting into a breeze, it's possible to accumulate loose coils as the line is wound onto the reel. Overcome this by running the line through the fingers of the rod-holding hand to apply even pressure to the line about every 20 casts.

EASY PULL: A dangling, loose line coil is easy to remove if you reduce drag tension, then pull line off the spool by pulling it through the spinning reel's line roller. With this technique, the top coils of line are pulled at a 90-degree angle to the underlying loose coils. When the loose coil is exposed, it untangles itself, or may need minimal fussing to fully clear it.

Braided lines are tough enough to resist abrasion when fish rub the line against a dock piling or rocks, and can be a tough line to cut when trimming knots. Owner, the hook company, markets Super Cut Scissors made especially for effortlessly cutting fine-diameter braided lines. These compact scissors are extremely sharp, and made of stainless steel so they won't rust. Comfortable handles are easy to grab and a padded pouch makes for easy storage. This is a must-have item for everyone who fishes braided lines. Alternatives are the blunt-point stainless steel or titanium scissors manufactured by Gerber and others as "kid-proof." They won't poke holes in your waders and they slip nicely into a shirt pocket. They're sold at office supply stores, fabric and sewing stores and craft stores.

CHOOSE YOUR COLOR

The opposing goals of line color are to make it invisible to the fish, or highly visible to the angler. Clear lines are a common choice, but pink, moss green and pale blue are also stealthy colors. Clear lines are so good at disappearing, that for some types of fishing, a hi-vis line is a better choice. Offshore trollers keep track of the baits and lures in the trolling pattern by following the brightly colored lines. Surf and jetty fishermen, and back-bay inshore anglers, are also using hi-vis lines in low light situations so they always have a visual reference to their line. The most popular colors are vivid yellow, electric blue, neon green and flame red. One of my favorites is the Sufix fluorescent orange for low-light fishing at dawn and dusk. Yep, the fish can see these lines too, but a 2- to 4-foot length of clear leader solves that problem for inshore fishing, while the lure's leader accomplishes the same result offshore.

A REAL SHOCKER

At the last instant when you get eyeball to eyeball with your striper, redfish, weakfish, tarpon, snook or big, bad bluefish, a shock leader can make the difference between netting a trophy catch, or telling a sad story to your buddies back at the dock. A shock leader is essential for the light-tackle angler because a brief rub of mono against a gill plate or against the chine of the boat, or a quick end-run around the outboard, can all happen in an instant. With no leader, the line can part with a painful snap!—and the fish is gone.

I recall a 30-pound class striper I hooked under a bridge on the backside of Ocean City, New Jersey that twice ran me into the pilings. A firm drag and a hard pull against a severely bent rod hauled the fish away and the 40-pound mono leader, although badly

Gamefish with raspy teeth like snook, striped bass, ladyfish, and acrobatic tarpon require a heavy leader to prevent the line from chafing.

scraped and frayed, held just fine. Without that leader, my 15-pound test main line would not have stood up to the abrasions and this fish tale would have had a sad ending.

As a general rule of thumb, the leader is usually two to three times the strength of the main fishing line. If your reel is packed with 12-pound test mono (or the equivalent diameter braid), use a 20 or 30-pound shock leader. A reel filled with 8-pound line would be best served with a 15-pound test leader.

There's also the ultimate shock leader, which uses 50- to 100-pound mono to guard against cut-offs from toothy critters like bluefish and Spanish mackerel, or from severe chafing by raspy mouths of trophy-size stripers, the biggest kind of snook and medium to large tarpon.

For maximum toughness and abrasion resistance, fluorocarbon gets the nod from most veteran light-tackle sharpies, but there are several monofilament lines available that are specially formulated to withstand the scrapes and rubs you'll encounter while fishing—and, these lines make good leaders. Examples are Ande, Trilene XT, original Stren, Hi-Seas Grand Slam and Shakespeare Supreme, and there are blends such as Berkley Vanish, Yo-Zuri and P-Line FluoroClear that also perform well as leaders. When using a mono-type line, it's a good idea to use the same brand leader as the line installed on the reel. You'll find that the knots will snug up much more readily because the line's basic chemical formulation, its surface slickness and its limpness characteristics are all the same. Knots will slide up nice and tight with little effort, only a slight bit of saliva needed for lubrication.

The length of the leader is open to debate. I've fished with guides who used a leader long enough to get a few wraps on the reel when the lure was reeled to within a few inches below the rod tip. Leaders of 7 or 8 feet in length offer the added benefit of reducing the strain on the main fishing line during periods of extended casting. However, the knot that joins the leader to the line can occasionally pull a coil or two of underlying line during the cast and cause a snarl; very bad news. For most back-bay fishing, a leader of 2 to 4 feet is usually adequate, and 3 to 5 feet for most inshore fishing. In clear water you may want to go a bit longer than when fishing cloudy or discolored water.

When fishing with mono as my main line, I use the same basic leader system Mark Sosin showed me many years ago because it's quick to tie and requires only a nail clipper to trim the knots, something I always have hanging around my neck when wading or hanging on a cord at the console of my skiff. The knots are simple

Bite leaders are essential when fishing with light mono lines or to make super braid lines less visible at the lure end. A mono or fluorocarbon leader can be joined to the main line with a two-turn surgeon's knot when joining mono to mono, or a five-turn surgeon's knot when joining braid to mono.

and can be tied even in low light at dawn or dusk, and I can even tie them at night by feel. At the end of the main fishing line I tie a 2-foot Spider hitch and add the mono leader with a double surgeon's knot. A Bimini twist is Mark Sosin's preference and can be substituted for the Spider hitch.

Why tie the Spider hitch (or a Bimini) before tying the surgeon's knot? Easy answer; the surgeon's knot tests out at about 80 to 90 percent of the unknotted line, so if tied directly to the main line, it weakens it substantially. The main fishing line must first be "built up" to be stronger. To put some meat on its bones, the mainline is doubled by tying the Spider hitch, one of those rare knots that doesn't lose any strength so at the knot it is just as strong as the unknotted line. The Spider hitch forms a length of doubled line, which is twice the strength of the main fishing line. When the surgeon's knot is used to add the leader, even though it slightly weakens the line, the weak point is now still stronger than the main fishing line.

For example, let's say we used 8-pound mono on the reel. At the Spider hitch, the line loses no strength, so the knot tests at 8 pounds. The Spider hitch forms a length of doubled line, and the combined strength of the two legs tests out at 16 pounds. When we add a 20-pound test leader, the surgeons knot weakens the double line only slightly to about 15 pounds, which is still far stronger than the 8-pound test main fishing line.

A blood knot or double uni-knot could also be used to add the leader. With either knot, tie a Spider hitch at the end of the main fishing line. Then marry the doubled up lighter line to the heavier leader. Both knots are a little trickier to tie, especially in low light situations, but are good substitutes for the surgeons knot.

When using a braided line as the main fishing line, I don't bother with the Spider hitch, but I do double about 3 feet of the braided line, lay it next to the mono or fluorocarbon leader and then tie a five-turn surgeon's knot. When pulled tight (use gloves so you don't cut your hands on the braid) this connection is virtually 100 percent as strong as the unknotted line. It's a simple, easy-to-tie knot that is exceptionally strong and its small diameter passes through guides without a snag.

To build a super shock leader, rely on the slim beauty knot to join the light and the heavy section. Its origins can be traced to Florida Keys tarpon guides in need of a strong, quick-to-tie knot, and it works just great anywhere along the coast. For maximum strength with very light lines, tie a Spider hitch or a Bimini twist at the end of the main line to double it. The double line is not essential, so tying direct is just fine for most fishing situations where you are using 8- to 30-pound test main line.

WHAT ABOUT WIRE?

For many years single-strand wire was the only effective choice to add a wire trace at the end of mono line, but there are many better choices, such as the uniquely flexible braided stainless steel wire from American Fishing Wire called Surflon Micro Supreme. This stuff is so flexible it can tie a clinch knot and a non-slip loop knot—yes, in wire.

Toothy critters like bluefish, barracuda, Atlantic bonito, inshore sharks, and king and Spanish mackerel call for 60- to 80-pound mono leader or a knottable wire like Surflon Micro Supreme.

The trick is to only pull on the tag end when tying a knot, not the standing part of the knot. If you do so, the wire will deform into a curly-cue shape that will hinder the lure action or its natural presentation.

Knottable wire is also available from Malin as BOA Wire and from Tyger-Wire. Surflon Micro Supreme is offered in many breaking strength ratings with 20-, 26- and 40-pound test the most frequently used.

GOOD KNOTS

Plenty has already been written about good knots, and there are numerous books on the subject at book stores and tackle shops; including *The Pocket Guide to Fishing Knots* and *The Really Useful Little Book of Knots* from Burford Books, and written by Peter Owen. All the line manufacturers have good knot-tying brochures, or you can visit their websites for a quick review of the best knots. Two of the best are Ande and Maxima (www.andemonofilament.com and *www.maxima-lines.com*). Lefty Kreh's *Fishing Knots* is another excellent book, especially for light tackle and fly fishing.

So, with all that is written, I'm not going to go crazy here with a laundry list of knots and illustrations; only those few that I use virtually every day that I'm fishing. The only knot that is relatively new here is the slim beauty. It has not had much exposure in fishing magazines and books, but it's a valuable knot to know.

Always wet the knots with saliva to lubricate them before cinching down tight. Always pull the knot with a quick but steady, even pressure—do not jerk the line or the knot may jam and become weakened.

Need a third hand? Install a brass cup holder at the edge of your workbench so you can pull hard as you need to when drawing the knot tight. On my boat console, a stainless steel U-cleat works just fine for the same purpose.

Improved Clinch Knot

This is an excellent knot for attaching a hook or snap to the leader or a swivel to the main fishing line, especially when rigging the Texas and Carolina rigs, wacky rigs, tying up shads for shad rigs and surf teasers.

It's quick and easy to tie, and when tied carefully it is about 95 percent of the strength of the unknotted line. Its strength is influenced by the number of turns and particularly by the insertion of the tag end back into the open loop. That extra tuck is what makes the knot "improved" over the standard clinch knot which has a bad reputation for slipping. In mono lines of 30-pound test or less, be sure to make five turns, but in lines of 40-pound test and above make three turns.

Start the clinch knot by (1) passing the line through the eye of the hook, snap or lure, double it back and make five turns around the standing line. Hold the coils in place and push the tag end through the first loop next to the eye, and then through the large loop. (2) Lubricate with saliva and draw the knot tight, being sure the coils do not overlap one another.

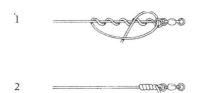

Improved Clinch Knot

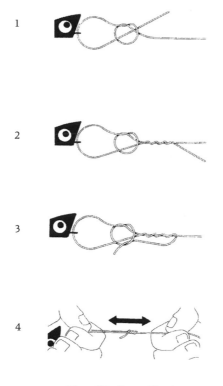

Non-Slip Loop Knot

Non-Slip Loop Knot

When you need maximum lure action, this is the knot of choice. It is reliable and tests at about 95 percent of the line's unknotted strength. When tied correctly the tag end faces toward the lure so this knot is less of a weed catcher than the improved clinch. It can be tied in any leader from 12- to 50-pound test with relative ease. Be sure to pull it tight and use pliers if needed to pull the tag end tight so there are no loose coils.

When sizing the loop, remember that the smaller the overhand knot, the smaller the loop will be.

To tie the non-slip loop knot, (1) tie an overhand knot in the leader, draw it down snug but not tight, pass the tag end through the eye of the hook, snap or lure and then through the overhand knot on the same side that the leader exited the overhand knot, as shown in the illustration. (2) Make five turns around the standing line, and then (3) push the tag end through the overhand knot on the same side as the line exited the knot. Complete the knot 4) by first tightening the overhand knot, then pull both the tag end and the standing line to draw the coils closed.

Surgeon's Knot

An old-time favorite for joining a heavy leader to the main fishing line, the surgeon's knot is reliable and relatively strong testing at about 85 percent of the line's strength. For maximum strength, tie a Spider hitch in the main line before bending it to the leader with the surgeon's knot.

It is also a strong, slim-profile knot for joining a mono or fluorocarbon leader to super braid if that's your main line. Use four or five turns, then pull tight. The braided line should be doubled.

The surgeon's knot is quick and simple. (1) When joining mono to mono, lay the line and leader next to one another overlapping by about 8 to 12 inches. (2) Make on overhand knot as if the line and leader are one, then (3) pass the line and leader through the overhand loop one more time. (4) Lubricate with saliva and draw tight. Note: When joining a mono leader to braided line it is important to pass the two lines through the loop five to seven times.

1

2

3

4

Surgeon's Knot

Spider Hitch

The Spider hitch is the simplest, quickest way to make a double line in monofilament—this knot can even be tied at night simply by feel. It tests out at 100 percent of the line's unknotted strength, but under extreme conditions of constant flexing it may weaken and lose up to 10 percent of its strength. The Spider hitch is an excellent alternative to the Bimini twist, especially with lines testing 20 pounds or less.

Start the Spider hitch by (1) folding about 14 to 16 inches of line to form a double line and then make a loop. (2) Hold the loop between the thumb and forefinger with the thumb extended well beyond the forefinger. (3) Wind the double line five times around the extended thumb and pass the tag end through the open loop. (4) Pull the tag end of the double line through the loop, allowing the coils to slide off the thumb. (5) Lubricate and draw tight.

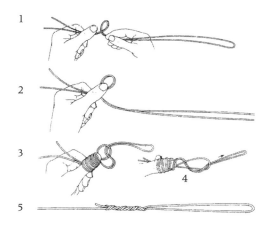

1

2

3

4

5

Spider Hitch

Slim Beauty

For many fishermen the slim beauty has replaced the Albright knot as the essential connection between the main fishing line and a very heavy shock leader. It's simple to tie with only a little practice, and it's very strong. A huge advantage is the knot's slim profile that slips through guides with no hang ups, as often happens with bulkier knots. The slim beauty can also be used to join a braided line to a heavy leader.

To tie the slim beauty, (1) begin by tying a double overhand loop in the leader, and draw it down until it collapses and looks like a figure eight. (2) Pass the tag end of the doubled over main fishing line through the small loops on the right and left side of the figure eight of the leader. (3) Make five turns away from the figure eight, (4) then make three more turns in reverse back toward the figure eight. To finish the knot, (5) pass the tag end through the small gap between the figure eight and the first forward wrap of the doubled line. Lubricate and draw tight being careful that the coils of the double line do not overlap one another. Pliers are usually needed to pull firmly on the short tag end of the heavy leader.

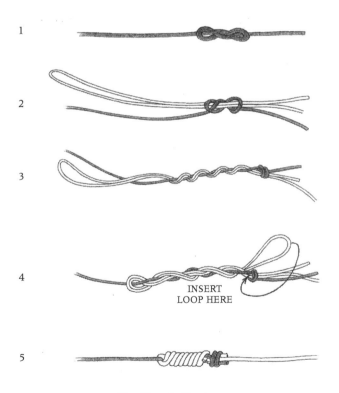

Slim Beauty Knot

DOWN AND DIRTY TACTICS

At the strike, a short, sharp lift of the rod tip will usually set the hook if the hooks are sharp. Here's another time when a rod with some backbone will help get the job done. A wimpy action rod will not properly set the hook. A braided line is also a big help because it has virtually no stretch. Once hooked up, the fish will be in control for a short while, so let him run if you're in open water—that's part of the fun!

Although the classic pose of an angler battling a fish is with the rod held with the tip high and pointing skyward, this is really the least effective way to fight the fish—in fact, it's the cause of many rod failures. A better strategy that delivers a quicker knockout punch is the down and dirty rod technique with the rod held low and at no more than 45 degrees to the fish. It's most effective when the rod is held low and parallel to the water and in the opposite direction the fish is running. If a scrappy striper heads left away from the boat on a fast run, hold the rod low and to the right. Even a straight away run is best handled with the rod held low and off to one side, rather than with the tip held high.

The down and dirty technique forces the fish to fight harder, and expend more energy against the pull of the line and the bend of the rod, thus tiring more quickly. This shortens the length of the fight and assures that the fish will be released without being totally exhausted by fatigue.

Eagle Claw's Chris Russell puts the boots to a hefty snook by holding the rod tip low and to the side. This down and dirty technique applies maximum pressure against the fish.

Applying power against the fish is the primary reason why 7-foot medium action rods with a powerful butt section are employed. A rod with no backbone has minimal power to fight the fish. The angler is simply holding on while the fish does its thing. Because a wimpy rod has very little power, the fish is played to exhaustion and when released, is a prime candidate for the mortuary.

Another classic fish-fighting theme is to pump the fish in by alternately raising the rod tip to pull in line, then winding the line onto the reel when the rod tip is lowered. With very light tackle, pumping is still the game, but you'll get best results if the pumping action is done with carefully applied short strokes. Work the rod down and dirty to the side, and use a short haul or sweep of the rod tip, then gain a half crank on the reel as the rod is relaxed. Although only a short length of line is gained each time, repeated quick applications of this technique will bring the fish to the net much faster than the more dramatic long sweeps of the rod tip.

Old hands at light-tackle fishing know that a lot of pressure can be applied to tire a fish even when fishing with relatively light line. The trick is to make sure you are using all the drag that you can. With 12-pound test, use 4 pounds of drag, and test this setting with an accurate hand scale to become familiar with the way 4 pounds of drag feels when the line is pulled from the reel. If you have never used a scale to set the drag, you'll probably be amazed at how firmly 4 pounds of drag feels, and you'd swear that the drag was set at substantially more than 4 pounds. Check your drag with a hand scale until you get the feel of the drag in your memory bank. To tire fish quickly, it's important to apply as much pressure as possible. Anything less and you are fighting the fish like a boxer with one hand tied behind his back.

Momentary extra drag can be applied to the spool with pressure from the finger tips of your left hand. If the fish tries to surge away, lift your fingers from the spool and the original drag is instantly restored. Slight added pressure from your finger tips can be helpful to "muscle" a fish into the landing net. Those last several feet are often the hardest.

10

FISHING TIPS, TRICKS AND TECHNIQUES

Numerous tips, tricks and techniques have been liberally sprinkled throughout these pages as examples of how to fish the many different types of soft-plastic lures. It's now a good time to bring together all these bits and pieces into one package, and to cover some techniques not thoroughly covered in earlier pages, such as back bay and shallow water, bridge fishing and surf fishing tactics. There will be some overlap, but I believe the brief repetition and expended details will be useful.

To become proficient with soft-plastic lures, there's no substitute for on-the-water experience. Guides and captains have tons of it, and that's a big advantage you gain when fishing with them. Whether it's Nantucket, Pamlico Sound or Indian River, a guide's insight into what works best, and the learning experience of how a pro works his tackle and lure retrieves, is invaluable. Booking a trip with a local guide or charter skipper when fishing a new area is smart; nothing beats a day with a pro for getting up to speed quickly.

You can also get a lot of good tips watching the TV fishing shows—once you get beyond the whoopin' and hollerin.' Watch how the anglers work their wrist to impart lure action with the rod hand, how fast they crank the reel handle and how they position the rod tip—high or low to the water. With rare exceptions, such as Mark Sosin, Blair Wiggins, George Poveromo and a few others, many TV shows are devoid of meaningful information beyond the name and location of the lodge where the anglers fished, but you can still gain valuable insights by watching what they are doing to learn how they handle their tackle and fight the fish.

Seasonal sport shows and seminars, and fishing club meetings that feature educational programs are excellent events where you can gain additional knowledge. Guides, charter captains and local sharpies are often the guys who are presenting the seminars and you get the chance to pick their brains for details and fishing tips, and to see first-hand the tackle, lures and techniques they are using and recommend. An excellent entertaining and instructional DVD titled "D.O.A. Lures, The Unfair DVD," is full of good information, some amazing underwater footage and plenty of tips. Check it out at www.doalures.com for details.

PAYING CLOSE ATTENTION

We've all experienced it; fish side by side with your buddy, using identical tackle and lure and one of you may be able to out-fish the other. Why? Well, probably it had to do with the retrieve technique—it can make a world of difference. How you work the rod tip and the speed of the retrieve are essential factors that influence how many strikes or hook-ups you will get.

Anyone with just a little crusty salt behind the ears will admit they've probably experienced both sides of success. It's easy to be a hero one minute and a bum the next. Fishing Connecticut's Norwalk

Islands and catching school striped bass one morning, I got smug after catching several fish while my partner, Ken Malvik, rang up a zero. "It's all skill," I jokingly told him, but after that I couldn't catch my fanny with both hands. Ken had been closely watching my retrieve, and duplicated the jigging rhythm and the speed I had used, and he began to catch bass after bass. "It's all skill," he said, "except for 90 percent luck!" As he rubbed it in a little, I had to ask myself "What am I doing wrong?"

While fishing a mangrove creek, Rich Barrett caught this tarpon snook, a close cousin to the common snook, on a pink and chartreuse D.O.A. shad tail nicknamed the electric chicken. It's a favorite color for striped bass too.

In my excitement I had quickened the speed of my original retrieve and increased the rate and speed of the jigging motion. Now I watched Ken, and once I calmed down and got back on track with a slower retrieve, caught two more stripers before the tide quit. Details can be important.

A similar thing happened to me with my buddy Jeff Merrill when we were targeting weakfish in Barnegat Bay one May morning looking for a shot at early tiderunners. My success was not up to par with Jeff who was catching two or three weakies for every one of mine. Jeff managed to score several nice-size weakfish up to 7 pounds on bubble gum pink Fin-S Fish. When I compared my technique to his, it looked like I was doing the exact same thing, until I noticed that he was using a spinning reel one size smaller than mine. Even though we were reeling at the same pace, my lure was working at a slightly faster speed because of the larger spool diameter.

I had another rod and reel in the console rod holder that matched Jeff's outfit, and after I made the switch, I began to catch more fish. It's incredible how such a small difference can make or break your success, but that minimal retrieve variation was all it took for me to get back on track and put together a good catch of tiderunners.

Back in chapter 4, several basic retrieve styles were discussed; do-nothing, steady regular, erratic, hopping and vertical. The principals of these retrieves can be applied to all other soft baits, such as worms, jerk-baits, squids and twirly tails rigged Texas and Carolina style, or fished weightless, and not just leadheads. No matter which lure is selected, the steady regular retrieve rhythm is usually the most productive, just as with leadheads, but an erratic retrieve can also be effective at times.

Equally important as the style of retrieve, the angler must develop a "feel" for the retrieve. What is the retrieve "feel?" That's tough to describe; much like asking someone to describe the taste of an apple or the aroma of fresh coffee. Perhaps describing what happens during the retrieve has more value. The angler will catch more fish if he can feel the wiggle of the lure's tail, the bounce along the bottom or soft pull of the lure against the rod tip. Just as you hold the lure in your hand, you must develop a feel for the lure held at the end of the rod, reel and line.

Experience is the best teacher, concentration is the best tool. Ever fish with someone who jabbers all day long instead of paying attention to his fishing? We all have, and I don't mean to suggest that we can't talk, but too much conversation steals away from the job at hand; making that lure work like it's alive. One of the reasons I enjoy fishing at night is the increased intensity of the session, which is enhanced dramatically as the visibility goes down. You have to concentrate more on the cast, the retrieve and what the lure is doing as it works its way through the water. Anyone who fishes at night will usually become a better all-round day-time fisherman because of the special learning experience that comes with fishing in the dark.

INSHORE BACK-BAY BONANZA

New England's salt ponds, Virginia's coastal marshes and Florida's mangrove lagoons; the big coastal bays in Long Island, New Jersey, Maryland and North Carolina, and the grass flats of the Florida Keys have much in common. They are dynamic environmental engines producing enormous quantities of bait and food, providing essential spawning and nursery grounds for gamefish and vital sheltering areas for plants, wildlife and fish. For coastal anglers, these priceless natural jewels offer outstanding opportunities to catch many of their favorite fish, and the potential for fishing with soft-plastic baits is limited only by the angler's skill, the weather, tides and the season.

You have to feel it to reel it. Linda Barrett used a combination of concentration, sensitive tackle, and just the right jigging motion to fool this dinner-size keeper fluke.

At first glance a bay, especially a relatively small one, may not appear to have a lot of structure, but do a little investigating and you'll find plenty of channel edges, points of land, sand bars, holes, narrow areas that accelerate tide flow, jetties and a host of other fish-attracting areas. A fly fisherman I bump into every so often once said of the Manasquan River, a relatively small stretch of water only 2 miles long, "I could fish this river for the rest of my life and still never know all of it. Every time I fish it I find something new." I think he's right on target, and I've followed his philosophy at other good, but small, fishing places, often focusing on small stretches of water that I find appealing such as Hobe Sound, the Loxahatchee River and St. Lucie Inlet area in Florida. Small places have a fascination all their own and you can become much more intimate with them than with larger bodies of water.

To be consistently successful, tides and water temperatures are usually of critical importance. The general rule of thumb is that fish move in with the rising tide, feed through the high and get the most aggressive on the falling tide. Like every rule, there are exceptions in some locations, but this formula is always a good starting point. Gamefish will move with the edge of a temperature break as the tide sloshes that thermal edge toward and then away from the nearest inlet. In Delaware Bay I once moved nearly 5 miles to stay on the leading edge of a falling-tide temperature break, moving from the Pin Top just northwest of Brandywine Light to the mouth of the bay at Brown's Shoal, just to stay with a large pack of weakfish. As the tide flow moved out of the bay, it left behind cool water. If you were in the cool water; no fish—zip, zero, nada. Crank up the Evinrude and head 200 yards to the new location of the temperature break and you were yelling "Fish on!" once again.

Most bays are filled with a good mix of structure, starting with the entry point of the nearest inlet. Many inlets are bordered by rocks to keep the inlet stable for navigation and these jetty rocks provide a great home for a ready bait supply and many species of gamefish, such as snook and striped bass, weakfish, jacks, bluefish and more. Wabasso, Florida guide Charlie Forbiano says, "The bottom structure, currents and land shapes around Sebastian Inlet are some of my favorite places for tarpon, big bull redfish, snook and jacks. It's like a magnet that draws fish to it, and I can usually rely on this area to get some exciting fishing experiences for my customers."

Although any tide can be a "good" one, inlets are usually best fished just before the end of the high or low slack, or at the start of the tide change. The mid tides may be too strong to effectively work the lure with any sensitivity, but all inlets are unique and different so you have to invest the time to personally get to know your local inlets. In fast moving water, stripers and snook will tend to hold near the bottom and you will have to adjust your technique accordingly to get the lure deep. When the current is not so strong, gamefish will tend to rise and may be located anywhere from the very bottom to the mid depths or perhaps just below the surface. The time period of maximum tidal flow is not the same for every inlet. The new and full moon phases dramatically affect inlets because the higher and lower tides push more water through the inlet, thereby increasing the tidal flow.

Land-based inlet fishermen cast soft plastics from the rock piles, aiming the cast up and into the current so the lure sinks to the bottom as it is swept along with the current flow. A heavy leadhead with a long-tailed soft plastic usually tracks better than a short tail, the long tail providing stability, much like the tail of a kite. The right weight head is important, and a good rule of thumb is to select a head with enough weight so that when you cast at about 45 degrees up current, the lure will be on the bottom when it is at 90 degrees to you. Adjust the size (weight) of the leadhead until you can feel it bounce bottom.

Let the lure bounce the bottom and be prepared for the strike as the lure begins to rise when it comes tight against the line. This is the sweet spot where many strikes will occur; just at the end of the swing. It is important to avoid slack in the line. You have to have contact with the lure to feel it working the bottom and to feel the strike of a gamefish. I keep my rod at about a 45-degree angle so I can lower the rod to keep in touch with the bottom, and also have enough lift distance to set the hook. If the rod is held nearly vertical, setting the hook becomes difficult.

It's also important to cover all the bottom in front of you. Long casts are impressive, but the fish are usually quite close to the jetty rocks or bulkhead and it pays off big time to make a variety of short, medium and long distance casts.

From a boat, inlets can be fished three ways; at anchor so the boat is in a stationary, with an electric trolling motor to maintain a semi stationary position or by drifting with the current. Anchoring in a narrow inlet is definitely not recommended, but wide, broad inlets can easily and safely be fished at anchor outside the main channel with no problem. The current sweeps a parade of bait and gamefish past the boat. At anchor, the soft plastic is cast up-tide, same as if you

Inlets provide terrific coastal fishing opportunities with an amazing combination of deep channels, shallow flats, tide rips, shoals, marsh edges, bridges, drop-offs, and rock jetties.

were fishing while standing on the jetty. As the lure bounces the bottom, reel in slack line to stay tight to the lure, to feel it working and to strike the fish. To get maximum lifting to strike the fish keep the rod tip low to the water or no more than 30 to 45 degrees to the water.

Using an electric trolling motor offers a lot more advantages than anchoring or drifting because the motor allows the angler to stem the tide and hold steady to work the lure in a small area with several casts before moving on a few feet to the next location. By casting into the current, at 90 degrees to the current or down-current, the angler can work a variety of retrieve angles and water depths, and work the rocky structure from many different approaches. The all-important swing angle will also vary with each change in casting direction, another benefit that helps you fool more fish.

A combination of maneuvering with the trolling motor and drifting combines the best features of two techniques to deliver some impressive catches. Captain Charlie Forbiano demonstrated this one morning when we fished the St. Lucie Inlet for snook, along with Chris Russell of Eagle Claw. As Chris and I cast D.O.A leadheads with electric chicken tails along the rocks at the inlet's southern edge, Charlie made skillful use of the electric motor to adjust the boat's position and the drift speed to help us score on several good-size snook to 21 pounds.

When drift fishing, the lure can be cast into the current or at an angle to the current. In either direction the lure can settle down deeper in the water. If you need to fish the backside of the current, a heavier lure may be needed.

The area inside of the inlet, where it enters the

Chris Russell of Eagle Claw took advantage of the falling tide as it washed bait through the St. Lucie Inlet, where he nabbed this 21-pound snook.

river or bay, is often a very productive fishing treasure chest, helped by the surrounding land formations to create wide and narrow areas, deep and shallow structure that all combine forces to create swirling eddies and essential structure to hold bait and gamefish. The varying bottom structure, currents and land shapes will alter the current flow and create sand bars, channels, cuts and shoals that become gamefish highways. The incoming tide delivers roaming schools of gamefish to the nearby flats, mangroves and marsh sedges, deep holes, channel edges and creeks or tributaries; and the falling tide sucks crabs, baitfish, shrimp and forage from this same structure. Gamefish love it!

Shallow flats are exciting places to fish because gamefish will glide onto the flats on the rising tide, often showing themselves as shadows through the clear water, or with other visual giveaways such as wakes when they push water, waving tails as they root along the bottom, or with their backs and dorsal fins showing. Even in daylight, the fish can be aggressive feeders readily striking a soft-plastic lure. They are on the flat for one reason only—to eat. Although at night the visual excitement decreases, the audible experience is intense as snook or striped bass make loud popping sounds as they slurp bait. The intimacy of the night is just as exciting as the daytime sight fishing.

Depending on the water depth, flats can be fished from a boat or by wading, which offers the ultimate in stealth if catching big trout, reds or snook are on your "to-do list." Wade fishing is so quiet; the fish will often glide past you only a rod tip away. This also holds true for larger striped bass on the New England flats at Monomoy where waders can often get shots at bigger fish that are spooked by the sounds and presence of a boat. Sometimes it's not just bigger fish that require stealth; sharpies in Barnegat Bay leave their boats anchored at the edge of a shallow flat and get out to wade the shallow bars. Fish that are spooked by the slapping sound of the boat's hull become a relatively easy mark for the wading fisherman.

Your tactics for fishing a flat will vary with the type of bottom. Heavy eel grass will foul lures that dredge through the grass, but that same lure can be effective when fished on a clean sandy bottom. An artificial shrimp is a very effective lure on a shallow flat. At the end of the cast, manually close the bail and then allow the shrimp to settle to the bottom. The retrieve should be made with a very slow cranking of the reel handle and occasional flicks of the wrist to lift the rod tip so the shrimp gently hops off the bottom. Hold the rod at a 30- to 45-degree angle to keep the lure riding high in the shallow water. Don't forget to try the minesweeping technique that keeps the shrimp riding high and on the surface at a slow retrieve speed.

Addictive Fishing *TV host, Blair Wiggins, hoists a grouper and a cubera snapper he caught while fishing with Captain Paul Hobby in shallow water just inside St. Lucie Inlet.*

The same upward rod angle will work with small leadheads and swimbaits, jerkbaits and tube baits, but the retrieve speed can be increased from slow to moderate—just crank fast enough to keep the lure from digging into the bottom, but slow enough so the lure dances just above it. If you are encountering a lot of weed, grass and algae, try a little more speed and use unweighted jerkbaits and tubes to keep the lure just below the surface, but above the bottom weeds.

When sight fishing, cast the lure so it lands just beyond and ahead of the fish, and not too close or the sound of the lure's entry will spook the fish. You want the retrieve to pull the lure on a path that intersects with the fish just ahead of the fish's eyesight. If the lure is too much to the side or behind the fish, the cast is wasted; it must be in front of the fish so the presentation looks natural. Sight fishing is exciting wherever you practice it; Florida Keys, Stuart, the flats behind Virginia's barrier islands or New England sand flats. Jim Donofrio, executive director of the Recreational Fishing Alliance, often fishes his flats skiff on the crystal clear sandy flats of Barnegat Bay. "Flats fishing offers special rewards," Jim says, "the best of which is the chance to see the striped bass actually strike the lure. To visually see the fish, make the cast and then watch the take is a terrific experience."

Not all sight fishing on flats focuses on seeing the fish. Watch for dark and light edges where eel grass and open sand meet and where striped bass and weakfish cruise looking for crabs, baitfish and shrimp; or the sandy "pot holes" surrounded by eel grass where trout and snook will lie in wait ready to ambush their next meal. Even if you can't see the fish, the visible differences in bottom coloration are easy to see and offer good shots at many species of gamefish.

Flats can be large or small. The Florida Keys, the Indian River Lagoon and Carolina's Pamlico Sound have miles of them; Florida's Hobe Sound, Cape Henlopen in Delaware, Connecticut's Norwalk Islands and Nantucket Harbor have only a few acres of them. Still other places have flats only a few hundred yards long, but all these places can produce good fishing.

As the flats empty on the falling tide, your game plan should switch to deeper waters, such as the drop-off at the edge of the flat, a channel edge, deep holes and sloughs. All are good locations for gamefish to get comfortable and feed until the next incoming tide triggers the short migration commute back onto the flats.

Deep holes are like aquariums where bait and gamefish congregate. As a general rule, the deeper the hole the better the fishing potential, especially for bigger fish, but every deep hole may not always be so "deep," and a foot or two of bottom change may be enough to hold fish. One of my favorite weakfish locations is a river

Jetty rocks attract big schools of bait, and gamefish take up residence here to dine on the buffet of food served with every tide change. Many inlet jetties have deep holes or pockets that should not be overlooked.

island surrounded by 3 feet of water. There's a 15-foot hole on one side and a 4-foot hole on the other. Sometimes the shallow hole has all the weakfish and the deep hole is filled with 2-pound bluefish.

Fish a shallow hole much like you do a shallow flat, rod held at 30 to 45 degrees so the lure does not plow through the bottom. Work it with hops so the lure dances just inches off the bottom. Work the lure deep near to the bottom for stripers and weakfish, snook and trout; but work it at mid-depth for fish that are suspended above the bottom like bluefish, jacks and ladyfish. If the hole is deep enough for the fishfinder to clearly mark the fish, it will tell you the best depth. One of my favorite weakfish holes is about 18 feet deep and will usually have the weakies marked right on the bottom, and 2-pound bluefish will be clearly marked on the fishfinder at 5 to 10 feet below the surface. If you didn't carefully watch the fishfinder for those bottom-hugging weakfish, you'd think you were in a bluefish hot spot.

When fishing down deep in a hole, make the cast, let the soft-plastic bait sink and then retrieve with upward jigging motions of the rod tip so the lures dances and bounces along, or just above, the bottom. In a fast current, work the lure directly below the boat, vertically jigging it up and down as the boat drifts across the hole.

Sand bars, shoals, oyster and mussel beds are also terrific places to find fish. Their individual structure can be large or small, and some productive shoals may rise only a foot or two above the surrounding water, others may rise several feet off the bottom. Fishing with Captain Ed Zyak of Jensen Beach, Florida in a small cove off the Indian River, we encountered a dazzling display of speckled sea trout on the feed above a shallow ridge that ran only a foot higher than the surrounding water. The fish held off to the south side of the shallow rise and chased bait that, as Ed said, "sizzled like bacon in the fry pan" as it fled the marauding school of specks. The action was awesome and only needed a small change of the bottom structure to collect the baitfish and put those trout in a feeding mood.

Other bars and shoals are much larger, like Robbins Reef in Long Island's Peconic Bay, or the massive shoals at the mouth of Delaware Bay and the big, burly shoals at the entrance to Oregon Inlet in North Carolina. In theory they all work pretty much the same way; tidal current sweeps bait to the shoal, gamefish wait directly in front of, or the back side of the shoal, waiting to pounce on the next easy meal as baitfish tumble along in the current.

The deeper and more massive shoals can be drifted, or the engine of the boat can be put into gear so the boat stems the tide, as is the case in Cape May's sensational rips at the mouth of Delaware Bay. On the drift the lure is cast into the direction of the drift, at an angle

Deep edges along the channel drop-offs of the Intracoastal Waterway are prime spots for back-bay gamefish that move up onto the shallow flats with the rising tide, then drop back to the deep when it recedes.

to the drift or jigged vertically. When stemming the tide, cast the lures at 90 degrees to the boat so the lure sinks and is swept with the current. The strikes may occur as the line straightens and the lure swings. It can also pay off to cast towards the shoal and let the lure hold steady as the boat stems the tide, jigging the lure in the current and looking much like a natural baitfish.

Cuts in the bars are always fish attractors because the currents provide a direct feeding line as bait tumbles through these relatively narrow areas. One of my favorite shoals has a small cut between the sandy beach and the point of land that juts into the water. The shoal is about 75 yards long and covered with mussels. It's a great striped bass spot with bait and bass moving laterally along the shoal as the tide drops or rises, but the very best spot is the small cut that lies just a few feet off the tip of sandy beach. Strong currents flushed the mussels away leaving a sandy cut that becomes a baitfish highway as the dropping tide pushes masses of them through the narrow opening. Striped bass lie on the down-tide side feeding recklessly. They swim literally shoulder to shoulder sucking up bay anchovies like water-borne vacuum cleaners. The action is fierce just before low slack tide and then it's over like someone flipped the "off" switch.

Large or small, it's smart to fish the entire length of a bar or shoal, including the front and back side of it. The shoal may have fish located only at one end or one side and if you don't make a few casts to every yard of it, you may never find the fish and get a hook-up. When wading a shallow bar, shuffle slowly along the bar until you run out of shallow water and water is too deep to continue wading. Make your casts in a fan-like pattern right and left, and straight ahead so no water is overlooked.

It's amusing that boaters will cast into the shallows where the waders are fishing, and the shallow waders will cast out as far out as possible toward the boats. When wading, the fish are often right at your feet, so don't be in a hurry to make a record-breaking distance cast far out from the shore line. One morning in Hobe Sound I had waded quite far out onto a bar at low tide, thinking I'd have to get far out near the drop into deeper water. After wading the distance, a big pod of sea trout began to corral bait within a few feet of the sandy beach I had just waded through! I could only reach the fish after retracing my steps about 50 feet back towards the mangrove-lined edge of the sandy point.

The more knowledgeable you become about local structure, the more you can take advantage of the predictability of your favorite fish. You will get to know that striped bass, snook, tarpon, weakfish

Striped bass, snook, weakfish, and redfish can be spooked by noisy anchoring techniques. For maximum stealth and bottom-holding power, the author uses a spear anchor. It's super quiet and works great at night.

or trout, and redfish will usually be found at the edge of a certain bar or shoal at a particular time, tide stage and moon phase. When you have the fish dialed in like this, anchoring is a good technique to keep the boat close to the fish without disturbing them. The noise factor, especially from an outboard or electric motor, is eliminated and the fish become less wary. Unless you are dropping lures on deck and making a big racket on the boat, anchoring is a very stealthy way to catch fish along a shoal or bar.

Get into position a half hour before the optimum time frame so the fish get accustomed to the boat's presence. Avoid loudly splashing the anchor into the water, and shut off the engine soon as possible. When the bottom is soft and relatively shallow, my favorite anchoring technique is the Cajun Anchor, a stainless steel shaft that is plunged into the bottom as if throwing a spear. The Cajun Anchor (www.cajunanchor.com) holds with amazing power and is the most stealthy anchoring approach I've ever used, and it works in waters from only a foot or two of depth to 10 feet or more. It's a pretty cool set up.

An electric trolling motor is a handy tool to crab slowly back and forth along a bar, working lures into the face of the bar with little noise to disturb the fish. In shallow water, I often cast over the bar so the lure is worked in the back side, across the top and then on the front side. While this may seem contrary to a baitfish's normal behavior pattern, I have watched bait move randomly along a bar when the current is minimal to moderate, and I get many hook-ups with this technique when using leadheads and a slow retrieve speed with a steady, regular jigging action. If the soft-plastic has a paddle or curly tail less jigging is needed. At times I will pause the retrieve so the lure stops for a moment, letting the pulsating tail do its thing, then resume the retrieve. Many fish will strike just as you begin re-cranking the reel.

When casting from a position on the back side of the bar and into the current flow, work the lure slightly faster so it does not snag or burrow into the bottom. Front side or back side, casting in several directions helps you cover all the water possible, and gives the fish a chance to "rest." Sometimes after hooking two or three fish, the school becomes wary and may move off that spot a few yards to a new feeding location. Vary your casts to cover as much water as possible.

TIDAL CREEKS

Tidal creeks, cuts in a marsh and drainage gullies resemble inlets, only in miniature. The mouth of the creek may have a shoal, a deep hole, eddies and a channel, and the edges of the creek will have drop-offs, deep holes and undercut banks; and all of these areas are great places for fish to lie in wait for their next meal. They are the most productive at the falling tide as a buffet of food is washed from the upper reaches of the creek.

Gamefish will take up feeding stations at the center of the creek mouth where there is usually a channel or slough and the water is the deepest. Other times they may be located off to the sides where the water may shoal up and be shallower. The different bottom structures will cause eddies and rips to form as the water recedes from the creek. Their size can vary from tiny mangrove-lined indentations along an Everglades river to a Carolina creek lined with tall marsh grasses, or a New Jersey sedge with deep fingers cutting into the mussel-lined muddy marsh.

Larger creeks will be wider and project further into the marsh or mangroves. Some will have numerous turns as they meander toward the main bay and this snaking of the creek will create even more structure. Shallow points and bars are found at many of the inside turns while deep cuts are formed on the outside of a creek turn. Along the way, potholes, deep channels, undercut banks and tree blow-downs and stumps add more structure to the mix.

Drifting with the current, power drifting with an electric trolling motor and anchoring are three fishing options to effectively fish tidal

A shallow-draft skiff with an electric trolling motor helps you get into perfect fishing position without a lot of noise. Here the author uses the autopilot feature to work a marshy shoreline while casting to weakfish at the top end of Barnegat Bay.

creeks. Fishing a wide creek from a boat lets the angler cast to both sides of the creek to work the lures into every nook and cranny of the shoreline where stripers, snook, jacks, trout and weakfish may hold. Anchoring near a productive deep hole or drop-off can be effective with handfuls of fresh chum tossed into the tide to create an excited frenzy. An electric motor can be used to maintain steady position against the current, but when fish are located, I switch to a quick anchoring up with the Cajun Anchor system to thoroughly work that spot.

At the mouth of the creek, the current will often accelerate making drift fishing less of an option because the boat moves off the structure too quickly and repeated attempts to get back into position may spook the fish with the sound of the outboard engine. A better bet is to anchor or use an electric trolling motor to hold position. Casts are made into the current direction so the leadhead, swimbait, shrimp, crab or worm drifts with the current. If the fish are feeding on the surface, there's no need to let the lure sink, but if you see no evidence of surface fish, let the lure work the depths.

DEEP JIGGING IS FUN, SON!

Vertical jigging can be done in shallow or deep water, and it's a very effective technique to catch a wide variety of fish like bottom-feeding summer flounder, sea bass and grouper to wanderers like snook, striped bass, bluefish and jacks, and also pelagics like tuna and dolphin.

Because deep-holding fish are generally bigger than their shallow-water cousins, deep jigging is pure fun. The strikes are arm-jolting, the action is fast, and gut-busting battles to lift big fish from the deep cause muscle aches as pleasant reminders of good fishing. The technique has been popular for more than a hundred years. In the late 1890s, using tarred hand lines, Long Island Sound bluefish anglers fished from sailboats at the Middle Grounds off Port Jefferson with heavy diamond jigs and caught choppers until their hands were raw. Big bucktails have been used from Florida to Montauk to catch amberjack and grouper, cod and pollock, and sea bass over wrecks. Adding a plastic worm tail was just a natural thing to do, which brings us to today's deep jigging with soft-plastic lures.

Bucktails or leadheads dressed with a plastic tail are excellent deep-jigging lures. Leadheads and bucktails up to 8 ounces plunge to the bottom and are readily available at tackle shops. When draped with a soft-plastic tail they are hot stuff fished deep; so are big swimbaits.

When you're talking about amberjack, big striped bass, alligator-size bluefish and hefty snappers, the size of the fish can be quite large and they can pull like mad. Conventional tackle usually gets the

TV fishing personality Larry Dahlberg shows how to duke it out with a big amberjack off Key West. He puts maximum pressure on the fish with a quick short-stroke technique to lift the AJ a foot at a time.

"okay" nod from experienced deep jiggers, although there are some new spinning reels quite capable of handling big fish. Depending on the tackle, use a super-braid line of 30- to 50-pound test, keeping in mind that the lighter the line, the less water resistance and the better the jig will work, especially if there is a strong current or a fast drift speed to contend with. Braids also have no stretch so they are more sensitive to feel the lure, and the braid has the greatest hook setting power of any line; something very important when you are fishing deep water. Mono stretches, which diminishes its hook-seeking ability on deep water.

You'll also need a powerful rod, preferably graphite, with plenty of lifting power in the butt section. Using the short-stroking technique to gain line in rapid, but short rod lifts, will get the fish to the boat much faster than a soft rod. I prefer rods with a light, but not flimsy, tip and a heavy butt action, but avoid rods with ultra-fast tapers. While catching amberjack at the airplane wreck off Key West, Captain Steve Rogers of the Spear One, said it best, "When a big AJ hits the jig, the rod has to have plenty of power to haul that fish up a few feet right away, or you'll lose the fish for sure."

Most everyone who seriously deep jigs relies on a conventional reel because it has greater lifting power than spinning tackle. Many conventional reels now have high-speed gear ratios of up to 6:1, but deep jigging is not always about speed; in fact a slower, mid-range retrieve is often the best choice so choose the reel accordingly. Many times in deeper a slower retrieve will be much more effective than a very fast retrieve.

When your fishfinder shows fish marked at all depths and scattered from top to bottom, a straight, reel-it-in retrieve is often the most productive with no jigging of the rod tip needed. With a conventional outfit, tuck the rod butt under your left arm and crank the lure in at a brisk to moderate speed. Watch the recorder to verify the depth that the school of fish is located. When scattered at many levels, retrieve the lure all the way to the boat. When fish are marked down deep, keep the lure deep by not cranking it in all the way. After 10 to 20 cranks, free spool it again to stay deep.

Color choices can be important. Dark colors like purple and red have virtually no color reflection once they get below 20 to 30 feet. Other colors like green and yellow have lots of reflective color even at great depths of 50 feet or more. You never know ahead of time what color will thrill the fish on any given day, but if you are fishing with a bright soft lure and getting no or few, hits, try switching to an opposite dark color. That color difference may make a big addition to your catch.

When you're starting a drift at a new spot, each angler should use a different color soft-plastic tail. Once you've discovered which color is the best, then everyone switches over. If the bite slows, try switching colors again.

If any one thing kills the action of a deep-jigged soft-plastic lure, it's a bulky steel leader. Good fishermen know that wire leaders are not usually needed when deep jigging, even when toothy critters are around, like king mackerel or bluefish. The single-strand or braided steel leaders act like an elbow and allows the lure to fold back onto the fishing line when it is free spooled to the bottom causing the hook to foul on the line. Most large leadheads measure 3 to 5 inches in length and this serves as a built-in leader. If you are experiencing cut-offs, try a short leader of Surflon Micro Supreme from American Fishing Wire. This stuff is extremely flexible and you can tie a loop knot to the lure and a clinch knot to a barrel swivel to attach to the main fishing line. Surflon Micro has a relatively small diameter so it doesn't foul on the lure.

A heavier mono leader, however, can be useful to help lift fish into the boat or to avoid fraying light lines on the chine of a boat as a fish makes a sudden lunge under the boat before being gaffed or boated. When using mono line, tie a 2- foot Bimini or Spider hitch to double the end of the fishing line, then use a surgeon's or slim beauty knot to add a 4-foot section of 20- or 30-pound leader. To join a braided line to the leader, use a five-turn surgeon's knot.

The fishfinder is the deep-jig fisherman's best friend as it peers into the depths to see the location and profile of bottom structure, the location of bait and the feeding level of gamefish. It's as important as a good rod and reel.

SHADS IN THE SURF

Bucktails and leadheads were always one of my favorite lures for fishing the surf and jetties, but I picked up some good advice from Shell E. Caris at one of his surf seminars that has paid off big-time for me each fall; striped bass love shads in the suds. Years ago when I fished Monmouth County's jetties several times a week, a 1-ounce bucktail and rubber worm or Mister Twister tail was one of my go-to lures for striped bass, and that combo fooled a lot of fish. My horizons expanded after listening to Shell E. talking about leadheads with shad tails, and in the past few seasons, the arsenal of rubber shads expended even further with the introduction of the swim shad-style lures first triggered by Storm Lures.

The original bucktail and plastic-tail lures emphasized only a few colors; usually white bucktail on white plastic, white on purple or white on yellow. With the advent of shad tails on leadheads, the palette of colors included chartreuse, pink, yellow and blended colors that added a more natural life-like appearance. Swim shads added even more realism with finishes that incorporated unique holographic and flash-foil body inserts and unique paint schemes. Many swim shads look so lifelike, you'd swear you were holding a real live peanut bunker or mullet in your hand. Only the hook gives the imitation away.

A Tsunami Swim Shad was the perfect imitation of a peanut bunker, and this teen-size striped bass just couldn't resist. Swim shads have become a go-to lure for many surfcasters. D.J. Muller photo.

I've talked to several avid surfcasters about their favorite color choices, and while each of them acknowledged the importance of the realistic finishes and their ability to attract gamefish, every one of them also noted that the white or pearl-white color was their favorite. One fall morning I had several bass on a pearl white Tsunami just before daylight, but finally lost it to a bluefish. I quickly added a replacement from my surf bag and continued casting; but with no hits for about 20 minutes. As the light of pre-dawn improved my vision, I noticed the replacement shad was not pearl, but was translucent and had a dark back. I switched back to a pearl white swim shad and soon had two more schoolies to add to the morning's catch.

The latest swim shads add another valuable dimension; profile. Swim shads can now imitate the silhouette of fat baits like mullet and peanut bunker, and also slim silhouettes like rainfish and sand eels. Some swim shads also add unique tail actions to gain additional motion and to emit fish-attracting vibrations during the retrieve. The standard swim shad paddle tail shape now includes curly tails and split tails giving surfcasters a wider choice of baits to throw.

The most popular swim shad sizes are the 4- and 5-inch shads which weigh about 1¼ to 2 ounces. The fact that most manufacturers only label their shads by length and not by weight is frustrating, but by trial and error you can figure out which shads will cast best with your tackle. Not every manufacturer's 5-inch shad weighs the same as another's, so one brand may feel just right for your tackle, another's of the same length may feel too heavy or too light. A little experimentation is needed.

The differences are not enormous, but even a ½-ounce variation can have big consequences effecting how the shad will run. Will it bounce just off the bottom or try to plow through the sand, or snag on a rocky bottom? I keep several sizes of swim shads in my bag to help me match the water depth. For instance, a deep-sloping beach can be more effectively fished with a heavier shad than when fishing a shallow beach where a lighter shad would be a better choice.

The position of the attachment eye, while similar on all swim-baits, does vary from brand to brand, and will influence how the swim shad will work in the water. An eye that is way forward on the

These surfcasters are working a quiet beach, reaching out with soft-plastic shads to striped bass cruising the drop-off. Plastic baits offer a wide variety of colors, sizes, and weights to suit most surfcasting opportunities. D.J. Muller photo.

nose of the lure tends to pull the shad on a shallow-running course. An attachment eye on top of the head will make the nose dig and the lure will run deeper. If the size is right, but if the shad runs too deep, hold the rod tip high to change the angle of pull.

Just as with the bucktails of the old days, little additional action by way of rod tip movement is required. In fact, less is usually more in this case. A slow to moderate retrieve with no jerks, sweeps or manipulation of the rod tip seems to be the most productive. Occasional, gentle rod lifts can help the lure dance in an up and down motion that can be attractive, but generally the straight retrieve is best.

If you are casting from the rock walls of an inlet, cast across the current and allow the swim shad to sink deep. Begin the retrieve as the lure makes the swing in the current. Most strikes will come at the end of the swing and as the shad is in the deep water.

Casting from a jetty can be very competitive if there are others on the rocks ahead of you; and of course everyone wants to rush to the end to work the fan. You can often steal a bass or two by starting at the base of the jetty and working the pocket on the north side, then casting along the edges as you work your way out to the end. When working the fan, keep the rod tip high so the shad swims through the rocks, but does not get loaded up with kelp, or snagged in the rocks.

Open beaches are ideal places to fish shads if you can locate productive beach structure. If the beach is scalloped with points jutting into the surf, fish the edge of the white water on each side of the point. Look for cuts in the sand bars and work these areas hard since these are the highways where bait and gamefish will move on the changing tides.

Sometimes you'll find cuts in the beach itself where the falling tide will create a river effect as the water level and the constant action of the waves washes out a hole in the beach. The waters a few yards away from where these "rivers" dump into the ocean are prime locations for bass, and weakfish too. The fish can be located off to the side of the current or right down the middle so the most effective approach is a series of fan casts that covers all the available water.

In calm water with mild surf, it's possible to cast on an angle that is nearly parallel to the beach. This may sound weird to those surf-casters who always look for extreme distance casting, but most nights and mornings the bass will be in that narrow band close to the wash, and so will the bait. Small swim shads can be worked in the most productive shallow water for a longer time frame when retrieved at an angle to the beach. Instead of making a cast at 90 degrees to the beach, make the cast at 45 degrees and place the lure in front of more fish for a greater length of time.

For dinner, an 18-inch striper is just perfect; but the chance for recreational fishermen to keep a small bass for the dinner table has long disappeared in the fog of modern management of these great gamefish. Today we are encouraged to kill the breeders and release the little guys. Go figure. We are left with the reality of having to release many, many fish in the surf, and if we truly respect and value the striped bass, we must release these "shorts" quickly and efficiently so they are in the best possible health.

One terrific advantage of fishing with swim shads is that most bass are hooked in the mouth area, not down deep; and not with a second or third treble hook snagging them in the eye or gill plates. Striped bass caught on a bucktail, leadhead shad or a swim shad are usually hooked in the lips or upper jaw and can be released with a minimum of fuss and delay. They are, therefore, good candidates for survival.

THE BRIDGE TO GOOD FISHING

If you want to increase your soft-plastic fishing success, fish bridges. Although they hold fish night or day, the very best time is not during the daylight hours when cruisers, offshore fish boats and jet skis pour out of the rivers and inlets, but at night when less-serious fishermen are home watching the tube. Anyone who fishes the night

Paul Gamba casts to a rip formed as the current sweeps through bridge pilings in hope of hooking a fall-run striped bass. Bridges are ideal striper hangouts because they hold plenty of bait on the changing tides.

shift knows that bridges hold plenty of gamefish, and these hungry fishermen time their lives to be at specific bridges at the optimum moon and tide to phase. They put as many odds in their favor as possible and their logbooks, if they would show them to you, would prove this.

There are hundreds of bridge-fishing opportunities along the coast from New England to Florida, many of them only a few hundred yards away from inlets. Others are located up to a mile up river, but they still hold an abundance of gamefish. North or south, depending on where you live, your bridge fishing catch will include stripers, blues and weaks, or snook, jacks and tarpon. To catch these fish, you need to choose the best fishing times, throw the right lures and make careful tackle choices.

For gamefish, bridges have all the right stuff; a buffet food supply, structure and current. The bridge abutments attract shoals of bait and act as structure by deflecting the water causing currents to swirl and eddy. Additional structure is found in the drop-offs into the channel, or in the deep holes and pockets near the bridge between the main channel and the shore line. All these facts come together in a heady brew of fishing opportunities.

The gravitational pull of the moon at the full and new moon phases will increase the height of the tide, which in turn increases the flow of water into and out of inlets. Both moon phases can be extremely productive when bridge fishing. On the downside, the mid tide stage can have such strong currents that massive amounts of weed will also flow through the bridge abutments making weed-free casting and retrieving almost impossible. The last hour of the incoming and the start of the falling are often the best times of the tide stage to fish bridges during the full and new moons.

Light plays a big role in bridge fishing. The transition hour at dusk as the light fades away into darkness (or at dawn from dark to light) is always a favorite time to fish. After the light fades striped bass and weakfish may temporarily go off the feed for about an hour until they become adjusted to the darkness. Then the shadows cast from the bridge lights will hold baitfish and the fishing activity renews until the tide stage is completed.

Gamefish will hold in front of and alongside the bridge abutments, but most gamefish will maintain feeding positions on the down tide side of the bridge. Although the current can be strong, the eddy that forms immediately behind the abutment has almost no current. Striped bass can hold here with little energy expenditure and be ready to pounce on bait the current washes toward them.

The boat fisherman definitely has more freedom of movement than the shore-based angler. The boater can move from one bridge piling to another with ease, but the movement of the boat and the sound of the outboard engine may spook the fish. An electric trolling motor can be a big help to keep noise at a minimum. It's also important to avoid making boat noise—don't let hatches slam closed or drop tackle and lures on the deck. To keep noise at a minimum, many bridge fishermen will anchor up tide of the bridge, or under the bridge to effectively work their lures.

Matthew (left) and Will Blackwell (right) had a great time fishing with Captain Mark Nichols (the Ol' Man, center), catching this barrel-chested black drum at the Roosevelt Bridge in Stuart, Florida. Their dad David Blackwell, snapped the photo.

The beach angler lacks the mobility of the boater, but has an increased level of stealth that can result in amazing catches. Depending on the bridge, shore-based fishermen may be able to fish from bulkheads, rock piles or get into the water and wade parallel to the shore, moving up or down current around the bridge pilings close to shore. Bulkheaded waters are usually deep, but many bridges have sandy shorelines and these shallow areas can hold plenty of bait and lots of gamefish.

Soft baits that imitate sand and blood worms, and shrimp and crabs can be cast parallel to the bridge, allowed to swing in an arc in the current until the line straightens. The take is often just as the line straightens in the current. Swim shads and leadheads are usually cast to the side, then allowed to swing in the current. Strikes will occur at the end of the swing, but it can also pay off handsomely to cast straight away in the same direction as the current, and retrieve a leadhead or swimbait with short hops and a very slow cranking speed. If you are anchored at the bridge, cast up current and let the lure swing toward the boat, retrieve with a fast cranking speed to keep the line tight, and work the rod tip in short hops.

APPENDIX

Soft-Bait Manufacturers

New soft baits are continually introduced and can be seen for a first-hand look at local tackle shops, or check out these manufacturer's websites to get more information on the latest products.

Barefoot Rods & Tackle, LLC
PO Box 450
Morrisville, NC 27560
919.596.5007
www.barefootrodsandtackle.com

Bass Assassin Lures
232 SE Industrial Circle, Suite A
Mayo, FL 32066
386.294.1049
www.bassassassin.com

Bass Pro Shops
2500 East Kearney Street
Springfield, MO 65898
417.873.5000
www.basspro.com

Berkley
Pure Fishing America
1900 18th Street
Spirit Lake, IA 51360
800.237.5539
www.berkley-fishing.com

Bimini Bay Outfitters Ltd.
43 McKee Drive
Mahwah, NJ 07430
800.688.3481
www.biminibayoutfitters.com

Boone Bait Co, Inc.
PO Box 2966
Winter Park, FL 32790
407.975.8775
www.boonebait.com
boonebait@earthlink.net

Cabela's, Inc.
One Cabela Drive
Sidney, NE 69160
308.254.5505
www.cabelas.com

Classic Fishing Products, Inc.
PO Box 121249
Clermont, FL 34712
407.656.6133
www.culprit.com

Cotee Bait Company
6045 Sherwin Drive
Port Richey FL 34668
727.845.3737
www.cotee.com

Crème Lure Company
5401 Kent Drive
PO Box 6162
Tyler, TX 75711
800.527.8652
www.cremelure.com

DeLong Lure Mfg
955 Joliet Road
Valparaiso, IN 46385
219.465.1101
www.delonglures.com

D.O.A. Fishing Lures
1253 SE Dixie Cutoff Road
Stuart, FL 34994
772.287.5001
www.doalures.com

Gambler Lures
1945 N.W. 18th Street
Pompano Beach, FL 33069
954.969.1772
www.gambler-bang.com

Gary Yamamoto Custom Baits
PO Box 1000
849 S. Coppermine Road
Page, AZ 86040
928.645.3812
www.yamamoto.baits.com
www.baits.com

Hogy Lures
PO Box 570
Falmouth, MA 02541
www.hogylures.com

Lucky Strike Bait Works Ltd.
RR #3
2287 Whittington Drive
Peterborough, Ontario
Canada K9J 6X4
705.743.3849
www.luckystrikebaitworks.com

Lunker City Fishing Specialists
PO Box 1807
Meriden, CT 06450
203.237.3474
www.lunkercity.com

Mario's Lures
PO Box 1363
Middletown, CT 06457
860.344.1009

Mann's Bait Company, Inc.
1111 State Docks Road
Eufaula, AL 36027
334.687.5716
www.mannsbait.com

Mister Twister, Inc.
PO Drawer 1152
Minden, LA 71058
318.377.8818
www.mistertwister.com

Panther Martin Lures
19 North Columbia Street
Port Jefferson, NY 11777
800.852.0925
www.PantherMartin.com

Sea Striker
PO Box 459
158 Little Nine Drive
Morehead City, NC 28557
252.247.4113
www.seastriker.com

Stanley Jigs, Inc.
107 North Main Street
Huntington, TX 75949
936.876.5713
www.fishstanley.com

Storm Lures
10395 Yellow Circle Drive
Minnetonka, MN 55343
952.933.7060
www.stormlures.com

Uncle Josh Bait Company
525 Jefferson Street
Fort Atkinson, WI 53538
800.BIG-BASS
www.unclejosh.com

Wanabe Outdoors, Inc.
1308 Hawthorne Street
Zephyrhillis, FL 33540
www.wanabe.com

Williamson Lures
A Division of Rapala
10395 Yellow Circle Drive
Minnetonka, MN 55343
www.rapala.com

Yum Bait Company
3601 Jenny Lind
Fort Smith, AR 72901
www.yum3x.com

Zoom Bait Company
1581 Jennings Mill Road
Bogart, GA 30622
706.548.1008
www.zoombait.com

COME ON, DO IT!

Democracy is not a spectator sport. You must earnestly participate to achieve the benefits of good government, and in today's world of repressive fisheries management, we are blessed with several terrific organizations that deliver our political message.

Many issues face us, such as government regulations that favor commercial exploitation of important gamefish. We are regulated into catching trophy-size fish for the dinner table as minimum-size regulations go larger, sacrificing valuable spawning breeders on the altar of fisheries management. Well-financed environmental extremists are campaigning to close huge ocean areas, while advocating draconian fisheries regulations with no tolerance for sport fishermen. The list goes on.

Fortunately, our interests are well represented by the following organizations. They meet and lobby with legislators and management agencies to protect the future of sport fishing and the recreational fishing industry. With your support the future can be promising.

You probably spend a lot of money on rods, reels, tackle, plugs and gear, and may own a boat or beach buggy. I urge you to spend just a little more to join one, preferably all, of the following organizations that are working so hard to make sure you and your family can fish next year and into the next generation. Don't let these organizations down—join today.

Recreational Fishing Alliance
176B So. New York Road
Galloway, NJ 08205
$35 membership
www.savefish.com

International Game Fish Association
300 Gulf Stream Way
Dania Beach, FL 33004
$40 membership
www.igfa.org

Coastal Conservation Association
6919 Portwest, Suite 100
Houston, TX 77024
$25 membership
www.JoinCCA.org

Stripers Forever
PO Box 2781
South Portland, ME 04116
Free website, no fee membership
www.stripersforever.com

INDEX

ABOUT THE AUTHOR

Pete Barrett has been writing about his fishing experiences along the East Coast for the past 40 years and has published over 1200 feature stories. His travels have taken him from New England to the Outer Banks of North Carolina, Florida and the Bahamas, and he operated the charter boat "Linda B" for over 25 years for inshore and offshore fishing from the Manasquan River in New Jersey. His fishing stories have appeared in *Eastern Fly Fishing, Fly Fishing in Salt-waters, Game & Fish, Marlin, Outdoor Life, Salt Water Sportsman, Sportfishing* and *The Fisherman*.

A strong advocate of tag and release fishing, he has won several national and regional awards for his tagging efforts, and he is a firm believer in conserving and protecting gamefish from commercial overfishing and overly restrictive, unscientific regulations promoted by extreme environmentalists. Pete is a representative of the International Game Fish Association and a member of the Recreational Fishing Alliance advisory board, and has served on several state and federal gamefish management organizations, including the International Commission for the Conservation of Atlantic Tuna and the original committee that developed the Striped Bass Management Plan.

His previous books include; *Trolling for Striped Bass and Bluefish, Saltwater Fishing Guide, Fishing for Tuna and Marlin* and *Fishing for Sharks*.

Pete and his wife, Linda, fish spring through fall for striped bass, bluefish, fluke and weakfish; and for snook, trout and southern species in the winter. Their son, Rich, is a full-time captain fishing from New England through Florida, Bermuda, Mexico and the Bahamas.